Brain Disruption

RADICAL INNOVATION IN BUSINESS
THROUGH IMPROV

Bruce Montgomery
and
Gail Montgomery

ExperienceYes Press
Evergreen, CO

ExperienceYes Press
6551 Arapahoe Drive
Evergreen, CO 80439
www.experienceyes.com
www.braindisruption.com

Book Layout: BookDesignTemplates.com
Cover Design: Erin Wright, Asylum

Ordering Information:
Quantity sales. Special discounts are available on quantity purchases by corporations, associations, and others. For details, contact the "Special Sales Department" at the address above.

Brain Disruption / Montgomery & Montgomery. —2nd ed.
ISBN 978-0692491829; 0692491821

ACKNOWLEDGEMENTS

We are deeply indebted to our clients and colleagues who encouraged us to write this book. Those people include: Wende & Brent Abrahm, Cristina Amigoni, Arthur Blume, Steve Brown, Meme Callnin, Jeff Carson, Alan Cohen, Linda Gallup, John & Jenn Langhus, Tom Miller, Dan Park, Travis Parkinson, Brian Peters, Josh Pinkert, Sarah Schillereff, Larry Siegel, Sara Steen, and the faculty of the Daniels College of Business at the University of Denver (including Charlie Knight, Barb Kreisman, Scott McLagan, and Kerry Plemmons).

We realize that we could not have gotten where we are without the support and sacrifices of our families. We are thankful for Peter & Betsy Montgomery, Jack Schnepp, Terri Schnepp, Cynthia Barclay, Steve Davis, Jack Montgomery, Paige Montgomery, David & Steffani Montgomery and Erin & Laura Wright.

Praise for ExperienceYes

"I was blown away by how ExperienceYes unlocked my team's creative power. We are a team of highly creative people. Still, to see the idea generation of our team at DaVita go up by 41% was just astounding, and I can see the value of using these skills and tactics in future innovation sessions."

– Bill Myers, Vice President, Marketing, Communications & Corporate Social Responsibility, DaVita

"We had a phenomenal experience with ExperienceYes from beginning to end, starting with the in-depth research they did to learn about and understand my organization and colleagues. From researching our business, to several in-person sessions discussing everything from personality types, leadership styles, challenges, and group dynamics, it was as if they were part of my team before they even arrived. I am excited to work with ExperienceYes moving forward in my hospital teams in many capacities. I cannot provide a stronger recommendation that you make them a part of your organization."

– Sarah Schillereff, DVM, Regional Vice President, VCA

"ExperienceYes takes leadership development to the next level. The facilitators encourage both personal and team growth at the same time. It was an extraordinary and innovative way for our Children's Hospital Colorado executive leaders to learn, grow...and laugh!"

– Nita Mosby Henry, Ph.D., Senior Vice President, HR, Children's Hospital Colorado

"We thought ExperienceYes was PHENOMENAL!!! Truly. You guys have definitely found your calling and what you offer people/organizations is so important and so great. Thank you for leading our team through your process! I hope to work with you again in the future.

– Kate Sparks, Program Developer, Executive Education, Daniels School of Business, University of Denver

"The Oil & Gas Industry is often a volatile and unpredictable industry. At Noble Energy, we strive to embrace creative thinking to make us flexible and agile. Bringing in ExperienceYes for our facility redesign project helped us to break down our existing thinking and get out of the "box" in which we were stuck. With their guidance, our team collaborated, innovated, and delivered solid results. We couldn't have gotten there without them."

– Brian Peters, Director – Major Projects, Noble Energy

"Kind of scary but fun and freeing! Gail and Bruce infused a new energy into the day (and week). I'm intrigued by how improv can translate into teamwork, better communication, and increased creativity in the workplace."

– Rocky Mountain Leadership Participant

MORE PRAISE FOR THE BOOK

"Brain Disruption practices what it preaches by taking an innovative approach to increasing innovation. With their 30 years of experience in acting and in business, Bruce and Gail Montgomery demonstrate how unleashing the power of improvisational acting can help people generate more ideas, teams work together more effectively, and companies compete better. Every company and every person who wants to be more creative, more innovative, and more successful will benefit from the tools and techniques in this book."

– Daniel Park, Chief Campus Counsel, UC San Diego

"The Montgomery team put science and art together in a tidy package called Brain Disruption. It is fascinating to see how understanding the neuroscience behind the creative process will help all of us get better at the innovation process. This book will be useful to our Executive MBA students as they combine the disciplines of finance, accounting, marketing, and leadership to build the organizations of the future. This is a great book for anyone looking to find the hard solutions to organizational aggravations."

– Kerry Plemmons, Professor of Practice, Daniels School of Business, University of Denver

"I can't wait to start using Brain Disruption with my team. I see this approach as our next way of staying competitive in the marketplace and driving significant change in our business."

– Josh Pinkert, CIO, Encana

"Innovation – any new idea – by definition will not be accepted at first. It takes repeated attempts, endless demonstrations, monotonous rehearsals before innovation can be accepted and internalized by an organization. This requires courageous patience."

– WARREN BENNIS
American scholar and author of *On Becoming a Leader*

Contents

Introduction

Never before in history has innovation offered promise of so much to so many in so short a time.
— Bill Gates

Innovation. It's a four syllable word that just rolls off the tongue of today's business leaders, right?

"Solve this problem."

"Be creative."

"We need a different way to do things!"

It all sounds SO easy.

But it isn't easy, is it? Innovation requires new ways of thinking. It requires ideas and ways to approach old and new problems – and then you have to get people to *accept* those ideas. And, more often than not, the process for generating and integrating those ideas into your everyday working life is devastatingly difficult.

We don't think it needs to be. At our company, ExperienceYes, we believe that you need to change *how you think* when you innovate to get to the next radical innovation.

Let's ask this question: Why do some companies innovate so well while other companies flounder? For every Pixar or IBM, there are seemingly endless Blockbusters and Radio-Shacks. What's the difference? What's the secret that enables *innovative* companies to release compelling new products and services? How do they always seem to have a leg up on the competition?

Over the last 20 years, we have developed a keen interest in innovation. We've consulted with (and been employed by) companies that represent a wide variety of industries: healthcare, manufacturing, software development, non-profit theatre, oil and gas, banking, insurance, education, and training and development. Every single one of these industries is looking for the answers to the same questions: How can we make products that people want? How can we do things better? How can we *innovate*?

In our experience, it doesn't matter WHAT you innovate, it matters HOW you do it. Innovation is a ***process***. Yet, surprisingly, there is a lack of good tools for teaching you the ***HOW of how you do it***. Until now.

That's where ***Brain Disruption*** comes in. Brain Disruption is the process of altering or shutting down the influence of the brain's "Executive Judge" – that part of the brain that tries to avoid risk at all costs. This area of the brain is an enemy to innovation ***because innovation takes risk***. Brain Disruption is a new approach to innovation that combines:

- Divergent Thinking

- Creativity
- Team Performance
- Corporate Culture

There is one item that is missing from this list, yet we feel it's the most important item of them all. It's the thing that we've discovered that great, innovative companies do better than everyone else. Innovative companies seem to always have endless ideas and to have ways to keep those ideas coming. How do they do it? How do they stay agile, flexible and responsive to a constantly changing environment? They use **IMPROVISATION**.

What is improvisation? Improvisation is the act of spontaneous creation. With it, you make something out of nothing, or devise a way to solve a problem without everything you expect to have. It's a process for saying "yes" to new things without the baggage of knowing the end game. It also happens to be the foundation for comedy groups like *Whose Line Is It Anyway? The Groundlings*, *Second City*, and *Saturday Night Live*. (Don't worry – we're not going to make you a stand-up comedian with this book!)

More importantly, through our research and experience, we've found that improvisation is a powerful business tool that dynamically alters behaviors and the brain. Through improvisation, you can create and establish an *innovative corporate culture* where anyone in a company is both allowed *and* certified to develop a new idea.

We are uniquely qualified to begin this conversation. We both spent the better part of a decade as professional actors in New York City, where we learned first-hand the importance of divergent thinking and improvisation. Later, as we developed in our corporate careers, we continued to nurture our passion for performing, ultimately starting our own improvisation troupe as well as performing with it professionally.

The structure of improvisation rests on four very basic rules: "Yes, and...," "Listen," "Support your teammate at all costs," and "Trust your instincts." Our experience with improvisation made us notice a serious skills gap in corporate America. Whether it was leading an IT organization, or implementing a large-scale software application, or trying to get a board of directors to actually take a new direction, there seemed to be no surefire method for getting people to think with innovation in mind. It was hit or miss. People **wanted** to innovate, they just didn't know **how to be creative or imagine a different path**. They were too worried about failure and the risks that always seemed to outweigh the benefits.

And then it hit us: **improvisation as a practice** was the perfect method for addressing that skills gap. These rules of improvisation could work as a business process for employees and companies, and therefore drive how people and companies innovate.

We started asking questions. Why are improvisation artists able to be so creative? How do they listen so well and respond so easily to change? Does the continued "practice" of improvisation increase the ability to be **MORE** creative? We didn't have the answers at the time. We just knew that there was something about improvisation that unlocked intense creativity.

We were inspired. We began researching improvisation and how it related to the brain. We discovered that there are techniques for disrupting your thoughts in a way that opens up creativity while suppressing that ever-present Executive

Judge of the brain. We're certain you're familiar with the Executive Judge – it's that nagging internal voice that tells you what you are doing is stupid or ridiculous. It's the part of the brain that's afraid of change and risk, the part that is most likely to run away from new ideas and kill innovation.

Through our research, we found that improvisers have a way of *dampening the effect of the Executive Judge*. They are able to enter a mental state where new ideas and creative responses happen "in the moment." Fascinating stuff.

Eventually, we asked this:

1) If we knew that this state of creativity that occurs while improvising could basically shut down the part of the brain that prevents new ideas...

   ...and...

2) Business were struggling to find ways to innovate...

   ...then...

Could these two things combine to influence innovation in the workplace?

Two years ago we launched our innovation consulting company, ExperienceYes, and have since worked with a range of companies, from non-profits to the Fortune 500. With them, we've been able to focus on team performance while creating an innovation practice and culture. This book is the result of that experience.

As we mentioned earlier, innovation is difficult. And, believe it or not, a large part of that difficulty is caused by that three pound gelatinous mass between our ears: our brain. We **want** to have new ideas and imagine alternatives to our "business as usual" concepts. We **know** we have to be agile to survive the natural ebb and flow of customer needs and new products. But we also know ***change can be painful*** and is often met with conflict and pushback – a struggle that occurs not just in our teams and organizations, but also in our own BRAINS.

Many of these feelings come from our own previous experiences. We've probably all received invitations to corporate brainstorming sessions that began with an email containing hints of desperation about next quarter projections. Or, perhaps there were those required workshops that focus on fun and interesting ways to help you connect to one another with offerings like "Teamwork 101," "Strength Building," and "The Art of Listening." Chances are that those sessions did little to influence us in the long term.

Brain Disruption is different. ***It's not an "event."*** It requires discipline, focus, and practice to free the limitations set by how we think – how our brain stores data, interprets experiences, and habituates our behavior.

Ask yourself these questions:

- How can you be expected to learn to trust your co-workers if you don't practice the delicate art of TRUSTING?

- How can anyone feel confident and safe from having their ideas judged when everyone in the room has a brain that can't stop thinking about RISK?

- How can a team be prepared to function when they have never worked together before, never had clear and concise direction from a leader, and never been celebrated for FAILURE?

You don't solve these things in a 4- or 8-hour workshop.

At a very base level, innovation stems from a new idea. Innovation is risk. Innovation is change. But you can't just come up with a great idea and expect that you can hotwire your brain into getting onboard. It won't happen without a change in the way you **think**. In fact, your brain will be running the other direction, trying to find a warm, fuzzy, risk-free place to hide until that crazy idea moves on by. It's just safer that way.

So what can we do about it? How can we teach ourselves and our companies **_how_ _to_ _innovate_**? We need to alter our thinking and at the same time change how our teams relate to one another, while also establishing clear rules about how to operate and collaborate.

We need to disrupt our brains.

Consider this book a recipe for innovation. The ingredients are not new, but the combination of ingredients is.

This book will help you:

- Learn the rules of improvisation
- Improve your creativity
- Alter your team mechanics
- Change how you deal with failure
- Increase trust throughout your organization
- Develop a process for having fun

And most importantly:

- ***Get your teams to innovate***

The book is organized into five sections. In the first section we explore your brain and how it both facilitates and prevents you from being creative. We discuss cutting-edge research that illustrates that people who are **more creative** are more likely to come up with **good ideas**. By the end of the section, we hope to have convinced you that, although your brain is exceptional at mitigating risk, you need to learn and practice skills that will begin to enable you to think creatively and innovatively.

In the second section we focus on the characteristics of great teams. Rarely are we tasked with solving a problem alone – most of the time we need to get into a team to make it happen (regardless of whether we're introverts or extroverts). What makes one team perform better at solving problems than another? How can we get our teams to perform better faster? We discuss Brain Disruption in more detail, and assert that ***improvisational collaboration*** is a foundational skill for any great team.

In the third section we take a deep dive into the ***rules of improvisation*** and how those rules can be taught, practiced, and applied in a business context. We describe the stages of team performance through which every team moves, from Forming (the very beginning stage) to *Performing* (the final stage). Improvisation *accelerates* teams through these stages.

In the fourth section we delve into innovation at the macro level by exploring organizational culture. An organization's culture has a direct impact on whether individuals and teams can spread their wings and innovate. Our experience at

ExperienceYes has taught us that innovative cultures often center on a single word: ***failure.*** Though it sounds counterintuitive, cultures that encourage and foster failure in an organized and consistent way find more success. This requires great leaders who have tremendous courage in creating a space for people to try something new and fail. Great leaders *want* their people to take risks – even if failure is an outcome. We also discuss methods for integrating innovation into your business processes and the importance of ***fun and laughter*** (and how improv can improve and influence these).

The fifth section lays out the components of the *Brain Disruption*
4i Methodology for generating and supporting innovation. The process requires that everyone practices improvisation, understands the components of listening, and is able to create something out of nothing.

Throughout the book there are numerous exercises and tools designed to help you and your teams facilitate new and creative thinking. To make these tools and exercises easy to find, they are marked with:

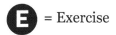 = Exercise

 = Tool

Let's be clear: ***innovation takes time***. Everyone has to learn, understand and play from the same rulebook before you'll truly see any major change. Companies like Apple, Google, and Pixar dedicate part of their business hours to creativity generation. This is not a "read a book and everything will work" approach. You have to practice, and to practice correctly you need a coach. We're that coach.

So buckle up. It's about to get interesting.

Section 1
Your Brain

"Rabbit's clever," said Pooh thoughtfully.
"Yes," said Piglet, "Rabbit's clever."
"And he has Brain."
"Yes," said Piglet, "Rabbit has Brain."
There was a long silence.
"I suppose," said Pooh, "that that's why he never
understands anything."
— A.A. Milne, Winnie-the-Pooh

Before you read any further, do the following exercise. Pull out your cellphone timer or look at the clock and give yourself two minutes. Two minutes exactly. Ready? Now, flip to the next page and over the next two minutes think of as many different ways that you can use a paperclip as possible. Go.

Different Ways to use a Paperclip	
1)	11)
2)	12)
3)	13)
4)	14)
5)	15)
6)	16)
7)	17)
8)	18)
9)	19)
10)	20)

Figure 1: Paperclip Test

Divergent Thinking

Ever take a test like this before? It's called an alternate uses test (AUT), and it's a common tool for measuring your ability for divergent thinking.

What is *divergent thinking* you ask? How is it different from creativity?

We like Sir Ken Robinson's definition.

"Creativity is the process of having original ideas that have value. Divergent thinking isn't a synonym. It's an essential capacity for creativity. It's the ability to see lots of possible answers to a question. Lots of possibilities to interpreting a question."[1]

With that in mind, how many ideas did you come up with? 5? 10? 30? Most people come up with around 10-15.

What if we told you that there was a study of a group of 1,600 people, and that 98% of that group scored in the genius level on this test based on the sheer number of ideas generated – that 98% were geniuses? What group of people do you think that would be?

The answer: **Kindergartners**

Why would Kindergartners be SO MUCH better at this test than you? The answer is quite simple: *they don't have the same boundaries that most of us do.*

Look at your list. Did you put down something like "to clip paper together?" Almost every one of our clients gives this answer. But why can't the paperclip be the staff used in The Raiders of the Lost Ark? Or a baseball bat that can knock the earth off its axis? Or a fighting stick for the world's smallest ninja?

If you change the size and material of the paperclip, and give your brain permission to let go of past restrictions you've placed on the object, there's a good chance that you could come up with many more ideas than just 10 or 15.

But we don't do that, do we? We are limited by our experience. We know the paperclip to be a paperclip, and our knowledge of the object itself drastically limits our thinking.

---

[1] Robinson, K. (2010, Oct 14). RSA Changing Education Paradigms. (RSA) Retrieved 12 30, 2014, from https://www.youtube.com/watch?v=zDZFcDGpL4U.

Kindergartners' brains, on the other hand, are WIDE open and can see no limitations.

The adult brain is exceptional at categorization. Life could be challenging if we didn't categorize objects and, instead, had to relearn what an object did each time we saw it. And once categorized, it's as if our brain says, "A paperclip holds paper together, and it will do so until the end of time."

Clearly there is efficiency to this type of approach. The National Institutes of Health recently mapped the entire brain using functional magnetic resonance imaging (fMRI). They discovered that the brain is actually organized like a grid – a vast superhighway of millions of interconnected neurons containing seemingly endless bits of data. The brain's connections turn out to cross at right angles, like the weave in fabric.[2]

We assert that this categorization likely allows us to travel down that superhighway of right angles to access data more quickly. It's like a major city – You want to find meaning of the word "paperclip?" Your brain "pulls out the map," looks for "Objects," turns left at "Office Supplies," then takes a right at "Paper Holders," and finally reaches paperclips! Voila! The location for the definition of "paperclip!"

But what happens when we need the paperclip to be something else? What happens when we want to re-categorize, or reimagine, that small piece of metal that holds paper together?

Let's talk about the Kindergartner study again. The researchers performed the study with the same group of 1,600 kids at different times in their development, starting in

---

[2] National Institute of Health. (2012, 3 29). Brain Wiring a No-Brainer. Retrieved February 8, 2016, from http://www.nih.gov/news/health/mar2012/nimh-29.htm.

Kindergarten and following them to adulthood. As the Kindergartners progressed, the data presented some interesting results (see Figure 2).

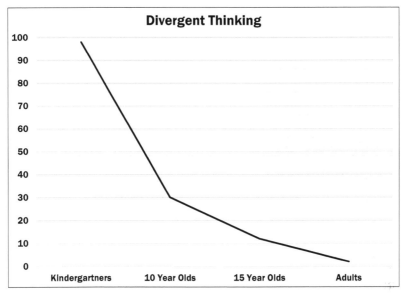

Figure 2: Divergent Thinking[3]

You'll notice that divergent thinking has a very strong trend downward. Think about it – 98% of people tested could come up with genius-level numbers of ideas for a paperclip when they were in Kindergarten. At age 20, only 2% were geniuses. Two percent.

If, at a very basic level, innovation = new ideas, then this drastic drop in idea generation is deeply problematic. So, the question becomes:

---

[3] Land, G., & Jarman, B. (1992). Breakpoint and Beyond: Mastering the Future Today. New York: HarperBusiness.

- *What can we do to disrupt the rigid and natural order of our thinking so that we can come up with radical new ideas?*

More Ideas = More Creativity

As we defined earlier, **creativity is the process of having original ideas that have value.** Those ideas could be brand new to the world, or tweaks to things that already exist. The important thing is that we need to have a lot of them. The volume of ideas (your ability to keep coming up with ways to use a paperclip, for example) actually matter. Why?

In a recent study at MIT, the number of ideas generated was directly correlated with creativity. In the first part of the study, 84 participants (students, professionals, and improvisational comedians) were asked to identify innovative product ideas for a common item, such as a toaster. The participants had only 12 minutes to come up with as many ideas as they could. Ideas included things like optically recognizing burned toast, and a cardboard box solar-powered toaster. The researchers then enlisted a separate group of people to rate the product ideas on five metrics: Creative, Novel, Useful, Product Worthy, and Clear.

In the second part of the study, the same participants were asked to create as many punchlines as they could over 5 minutes to a caption-less New Yorker cartoon (see Figure 3).

Figure 3: Sample New Yorker Cartoon

Responses included:

- The company is underwater...and we called you.

- We're expecting the stock market to go to the toilet and may need you for assistance.

- Who you calling beekeeper?

A similar group was asked to rate the legitimacy and humor of the responses.

Researchers then analyzed the results of both tests. What they found was fascinating – the respondents who had ***more ideas also had the more creative ideas.*** The researchers concluded that the ability to generate ideas quickly (the more ideas you had within the given time period) was strongly correlated to the creativity of those ideas (r^2 = .82).[4]

---

[4]Kudrowitz, B. (2010, September 10). HaHa and Aha! Creativity, Idea Generation, Improvisational Humor, and Product Design. Boston, MA, USA.

Or, put in another way, ***the people who had more ideas, had more ideas of value.***

Problems are solved by coming up with ideas. Sometimes a solution is simple and elegant, other times it is overwhelmingly complicated, but it does the same thing: it solves a problem. So it stands to reason that if we have a method for coming up with lots of ideas, then we are more likely to have an idea that will be good and useful – an idea that will actually "stick." Linus Pauling, the multiple Nobel prize-winning chemist, famously said, "The way to have a good idea is to have a lot of ideas."

Sounds simple, doesn't it? The challenge is that we get in the way of those ideas as we go from being Kindergartners to adults. We are so good at seeing things the way they ARE that we can't see them any other way. It's partly our makeup (how our brains are put together) and partly the way we learn. So the goal needs to be finding a way to shift the path of our brain's connections so we can increase our flow of creativity.

We can look at this as a process (see Figure 4). If you practice improving your divergent thinking skills, we've found that you can increase your number of ideas. Increasing the number of ideas can then increase your chances of finding something of value.

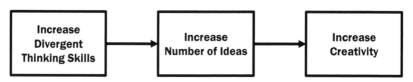

Figure 4: Divergent Thinking Process

Where does innovation sit in all of this?

To us, innovation is ***practical creativity***. It's the process of finding those ideas that have value, and then ***applying them to your business***. We will return to innovation later in this book. For now, let's focus on creativity.

Why Does Creativity Matter?

Now, you might at this point find yourself saying, "Great, I need to be more creative. But I work for a living, and creativity in business is an oxymoron. Or at least it is at my job."

We hear this from our clients quite a bit. Along with, "Shouldn't we just be making money and letting the Marketing team be creative?"

Recently, Forrester Consulting, a research-based consulting company, performed a quantitative study exploring how creativity influences business performance. We have always had a suspicion that creative companies outperform their peers (look at Disney, Apple, IDEO), but no real data to back it up. Now we do. The study, entitled *The Creative Dividend*, surveyed senior management from numerous companies that crossed both industries and geographies. The results of the study were astonishing:

- Companies that foster creativity achieve exceptional growth over their peers
- Creative companies enjoy greater market share and competitive leadership (by a factor of 3 to 1!)
- Creative companies win more "great places to work" awards (leading to higher retention rates and employee satisfaction)

The "creative dividend" is real. There are massive dollars at stake here when we're talking about a market share of 3 to 1, and yet 61% of companies do not see themselves as creative.[5] This leaves a HUGE gap (or opportunity) for a company to begin building a framework that is focused both on creativity and innovation, which in turn has the potential to drastically change its position in the marketplace.

Increasing Your Creativity and Divergent Thinking Skills

The good news is that there are lots of methods for increasing your divergent thinking skills. But be warned: it takes practice.

It's funny – In our workshops we find that our participants freely admit that to learn how to play a sport they need to practice. Think of how long it takes to become proficient at sports like hockey, basketball, or soccer.

"Hours on the field," they'll tell us, "You need to spend hours on the field." Yet, when it comes to creativity, or more importantly our brain, many think they do it just fine. They've got it down. "I know how to get this stuff done, thank you very much." Or, others believe that creativity can't be taught. Some people are creative. Other people aren't. It's that simple.

But it is possible to become more creative, regardless of whether you think you've got it down or it can't be taught. It's done with ***practice.*** Admitting you need to practice is the first step. You have to train your brain to think differently, and the brain will respond.

---

[5] Forrester Research. (2014). The Creative Dividend: How Creativity Impacts Business Results. Cambridge: Forrester Research.

There is a great deal of current research about neuroplasticity, or the ability of the brain to change and grow (regardless of age).

> *"Every brain is a work in progress. From the day we're born to the day we die, it continuously revises and remodels, improving or slowly declining, as a function of how we use it."*[6]

Your brain is malleable! It's a rich, dense and fertile ground that can be exercised and molded.

We've included a 4-week creativity and divergent thinking prescription in the Appendix called ***One Month Brain Disruption Training*** to get you started. It's a small commitment – maybe 5-10 minutes a day. It's necessary if you want to start the important process of altering and improving your creative abilities. Like hockey or soccer, time dedicated to improving basic skills will result in improvement over time.

---

[6] Merzenich, M. (2013, August 6). How You Can Make Your Brain Smarter Every Day. Retrieved March 12, 2015, from http://www.forbes.com/sites/nextavenue/2013/08/06/how-you-can-make-your-brain-smarter-every-day/.

Section 2
The Dream Team

"The strength of the team is each individual member.
The strength of each member is the team."
— *Phil Jackson*

Section 1 focused on you, the individual. How are *you* being creative? What is *your* brain doing when it's being creative? However, business does not happen in the vacuum of our brain. It happens at the office. With people. And those people are put in teams with us. And we're supposed to solve problems *with them.*

So, how do you take this concept of divergent thinking and apply it to a **group of people?** How do you get a **team** to work more effectively in a creative context?

We Built this Team by Picking Straws

Have you ever put together a team before? We mean *really* put it together, where you were thoughtful and could handpick each person for their strengths and input – like you were the head coach of the US Olympic Basketball team. Have you ever put together a team with the perfect distribution of talent?

In our experience, the process for putting together a team in the corporate world is far from Olympian. Instead, it looks like this:

1. Who has the time?

2. OK, no one has the time. So who's breathing?

Alright, admittedly, maybe it's not that bad. Or, at least, it's not *always* that bad. Teams, and their associated "collaborative work," have become the new normal for businesses today. Oh, sure, you can give teams other buzzword names – committee, task force, solution squad, application geniuses – but it's still the same thing: a group of people coming together to collaborate and get things done.

What makes a perfect team? Take a moment and fill in the following table.

Characteristics of the Perfect Team
1)
2)
3)
4)
5)
6)
7)
8)
9)
10)

Figure 5: Characteristics of a Perfect Team

If you're anything like our clients, you might have written down things like:

- Trust
- Know what the goal is
- Work together
- Communication
- No judgment
- Different backgrounds
- Everyone contributes
- Have fun

So, here's the question: **When was the last time you really focused on any of the items from this list?** We mean something beyond bowling, drinks at the local bar, or the annual Christmas party – rather, something that worked to fundamentally change the dynamics of how the team behaves, relates to one another, and develops trust.

You might be muttering to yourself, "Please don't tell me that you're going to recommend a trust fall or a ropes course."

We're not. Though those are both interesting ways to create bonds between team members. But, what happens four weeks later after those experiences? Traditionally, the team returns to their normal behavior and what was once a great shared experience fades away in response to the daily grind.

What else have you done to strengthen your team? Most likely nothing. Instead, there's an expectation that teams will simply form, work, and improve, with no real guidance or insight. And what does this give us?

Inconsistency. **Great inconsistency.** Some teams are fantastic and have positive outcomes; many do not.

Why is that? Inherently, you KNOW what makes a good team – or at least there are countless articles and books that can guide you. Good teams have diverse ideas and backgrounds, trust between team members, and share a common goal.

But, how do you **teach and practice** that?

Team Performance

We made the argument in Section 1 that creativity is important – the more ideas you have, the more you improve your creativity, the **more solutions of value you have**. And we just discussed the characteristics of the perfect team. What if there was a way to create an environment where some of those characteristics were rules that just so happen to improve team performance while at the same time increasing creativity skills? Wouldn't you want to *know* that?

We believe that there is one particular activity that disrupts the brain in a way that makes you better at being creative and better at performing as a team: **improvisation**, or "improv" for short. We mentioned in the Introduction that improv is the act of spontaneous creation. With it, you can make something out of nothing, or devise a way to solve a problem without everything you think you need.

Now, before you drop this book and say, "And that's where you lost me. I'm not doing that touchy-feely stuff," let's explore the rules of improv and the **neuroscience** behind it.

What do you think of when you hear the word improv? Our clients usually say something like:

- Fast-paced
- Funny
- Quick
- No boundaries
- Crazy
- Terrifying (and don't make me do it)

We think of the television show *Whose Line Is It Anyway?* a short-lived English production that first aired on the BBC in the late 1980's. It later came to the US in the late 1990's and ran for nearly ten seasons. The format was simple: one host, four performers. The US version was hosted by comedian Drew Carey and starred several gifted improvisers. In both versions, the host would provide specific situations (with random suggestions collected from the audience) for one or all of the performers. The performers would then "improv" their way through a situation.

For many people throughout the US this was their first introduction to improv comedy (though some may be aware of improv troupes like *The Groundlings* in LA and *Second City* in Chicago). The cast of *Whose Line Is It Anyway?* was quite incredible – truly gifted improvisers with a tremendous amount of talent. If you haven't seen them, go google a few of their "best of" collections.

Why were they so good? How were they able to take random suggestions from the audience and turn them into something that was exhilarating and hilarious to watch? How could they think so quickly?

The answer: they followed a structure that has clearly defined rules. Rules that, if consistently applied in a business context, would dramatically reshape how your business performs today.

What are they? (see Figure 6)

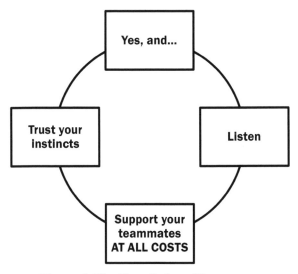

Figure 6: The Four Rules of Improv

Seen anything like these before? You might notice a similarity to the rules of "brainstorming," the technique first created through Creative Problem Solving and the work of Alex Osborn in the 1950's and 60's. Osborn introduced rules for brainstorming – like "defer judgement" and "welcome unusual ideas." You might immediately notice parallels to "Yes, and..." and "Support your teammates at all costs." However, with improv, you practice the rules *outside of the brainstorming session*, as opposed to waiting to when you're in a large conference room and expected to come up with new ideas. In this sense, improv is the ***ongoing foundation for brainstorming***, not just the event itself.

The researchers from the study out of MIT we referenced earlier found that:

> *...improvisational comedians on average produced 20% more product ideas and 25% more creative product*

ideas than professional product designers. Furthermore, the few individuals that were highly prolific in both creative product ideation and humorous cartoon caption production had an improvisational comedy background. Many of the games used in improvisational comedy training are intended to promote associative thinking. We designed an improvisational comedy workshop composed of these association-based games. A group of 11 subjects who participated in this workshop increased their idea output on average by 37% in a subsequent product brainstorming session. Our findings suggest that improvisational comedy games are a useful warm up for idea generation, that prolific generation is not a domain specific ability and that it is possible to teach creativity. Ultimately, this work can lead to the development of tools and methods that designers can use to improve their idea generation skills.[7]

We'll get into greater detail of the rules of improv and how they work soon. But let's talk first about the how and why of improv's ability to open neural pathways within that three pounds of mush between your ears.

The Neuroscience behind Improv and Creativity

We again have to return to your brain before we go any further. Your brain is divided up into many different regions that, thanks to fMRI technology, neuroscientists have begun to map and understand.

There is one phenomenal little part of your brain that loves to control things. Control things to a fault, in many cases. Although you may not be familiar with its name, we're certain

---

[7] Kudrowitz, B. (2010, September 10). HaHa and Aha! Creativity, Idea Generation, Improvisational Humor, and Product Design. Boston, MA, USA.

you're familiar with its behavior. It's called the dorsolateral prefrontal cortex, or DL-PFC, and it is responsible for some amazing things related to the executive functions of the brain like:

- Long-range planning
- Risk avoidance
- Working memory
- Inhibition
- Morality

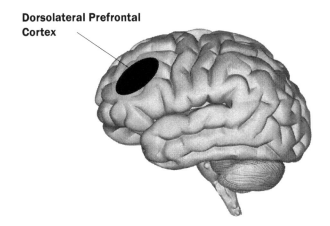

Figure 7: Dorsolateral Prefrontal Cortex[8]

The DL-PFC, or as we like to call it, the "Judge," came onto the scene pretty late in the evolutionary game and can be found in both humans and primates. Interestingly, it doesn't finish developing until we're adults – in the early 20's for women and mid 20's for men. (If you've ever wondered why a

[8] Brain Clinics. (2015). Dorsolateral Prefrontal Cortex. (Brain Clinics) Retrieved February 8, 2016, from http://www.brainclinics.com/dynamic/media/1/images/rTMS/DLPFC_Left.jpg.

teenager might make a decision on impulse without fully thinking it through, it's because the part of their brain that readily identifies good vs. bad decisions *isn't even in place yet*).

So, why is this important to us?

The Judge is great...except when you want to think of new ideas or be creative. It's the part of your brain that tells you "You're acting like an idiot," or "Why would you ever try something like that?" or "Whatever you think you're doing, it's too *risky*!"

Now, don't get us wrong. We NEED that little finger pointing, eye-rolling, restrictive part of the brain to function in society and to keep us alive. It's just that the Judge is NOT a friend to innovation, risk, and new ideas.

To put it another way: the Judge stifles creativity like a dog muzzle.

Maybe you've had the same experience we've had where you sit around a conference table and throw out ideas. No matter what the idea is, people around the table say things like, "No. We can't do that." Or, "That's impossible."

The Judge's natural response is to say "No" first and *maybe* ask questions later. It desperately wants to: 1) Avoid risk. 2) Avoid risk. 3) Oh, and avoid risk.

This is where folks like the cast of *Whose Line Is It Anyway?* have a significant leg up. When they improvise, their brains light up in the areas of creativity and dampen the Judge.

They are experiencing *Brain Disruption.*

Brain Disruption

Two recent studies have analyzed the brains of improvisers. The first study came out of Johns Hopkins and the work of Dr. Charles Limb. In that study, Limb took accomplished jazz musicians and imaged their brains during four tests. Two of the tests focused on memorized pieces of music (the C-major scale and a piece written for the study). The remaining two tests allowed the musician to riff (improvise) – first on the C-major scale, and then against a recorded piece of music.

The results showed that, when allowed the freedom to create their own music,

> *"...the brain turned off areas linked to self-monitoring and inhibition and turned on those that let self-expression flow. In addition, the brain regions involved with all of the senses lit up during that time of improvisation, indicating a heightened state of awareness — performers literally taste, smell, and feel the air around them. Most fascinating about this aspect of the scans was their uncanny similarity to patterns seen during deep REM sleep, creating a tantalizing notion of a connection between improvisation and dreaming."*[9]

So, a jazz musician who is improvising is able to quiet his/her Judge and allow the creative parts of their brain to activate. They actually suppress the Judge!

The second study came out of the National Institute on Deafness and Other Communication Disorders (NIDCD) in Los Angeles and focused on freestyle rap artists. Freestyle

---

[9] Zagorski, N. (2008, October 1). The Science of Improv. Retrieved February 8, 2016, from http://www.peabody.jhu.edu/past_issues/fall08/the_science_of_improv.html.

rapping is often performed as a battle on a stage in front of hundreds of people. A disc jockey (DJ) plays a beat-driven musical track, and each rap artist creates various rhymes off the beat. The requirement: the rhymes have to make sense and are most likely in response to whatever the other rapper has said. Through this process, the rappers weave in complex stories about their impressions of each other, their rap styles, and (occasionally) their mothers. The point is that it's all improvised right on the spot. (You can google "rap artist battle rounds" for examples).

Like the Johns Hopkins study, the rappers were analyzed under an fMRI. First, they were given a beat and asked to perform a memorized, well-rehearsed series of lyrics. Second, they were given the exact same beat and asked to freestyle.

The researchers saw a similar pattern in the brain of the rappers as compared to the jazz musicians. Take a look at the graph on the next page. You'll note that when the rappers freestyle, just like the jazz musicians, they dial down the Judge and dial up the parts of the brain that are involved with creativity (Figure 8).

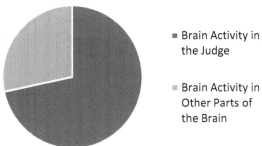

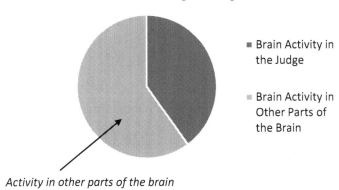

Activity in other parts of the brain increase while the Judge decreases

Figure 8: Comparing the Brain during Freestyled and Memorized Lyrics

How do they do this? Well, they have to suspend that part of the brain that's constantly judging, constantly telling them "this is stupid" in order to create something new.

Both studies found a positive correlation between a change in activity in the Judge and the ability to create things out of mid-air. The people who could suppress the Judge were better at activating the creative parts of their brain.

So, **how can we do this**? Again, we call back to the MIT study on improv from earlier in this section:

> *"We found that a group of 11 students individually generated on average 37% more ideas after an improvisational workshop."*[10]

You might be saying to yourself, "Great, but I'm no Miles Davis. I can barely think of what I should buy at the grocery store."

Well, what if you had a way of **practicing** the process of changing the dynamics of your brain? Regularly disrupting the Judge so that it gets out of the way, making those new ideas more readily available?

That's where improv, similar to the kind practiced by the cast of *Whose Line Is It Anyway?* comes into play.

Improvisational Collaboration

Think of the last time you truly worked *collaboratively*. We mean the kind where you were having a conversation that sparked an idea...and someone else built on that idea ...and then someone else built on that idea...and so on. No one was judging. No one was over-thinking things. You were just working together.

High performing teams play off one another. They listen and react. They DO things instead of waiting until things have been planned out to the "nth" degree.

[10] Kudrowitz, B. (2010, September 10). HaHa and Aha! Creativity, Idea Generation, Improvisational Humor, and Product Design. Boston, MA, USA.

What types of teams come to mind when you think of *collaboration*?

We think of the Japanese cooking show Iron Chef. The Iron Chef started in the early 1990's and ended in 1999. It pitted a master chef (known as an Iron Chef) in a specific cuisine against a challenger.

 At the beginning of the show the challenger would pick which Iron Chef they wanted to battle. Then, the secret ingredient of the day would be revealed. The ingredient would serve as the basis for four to six dishes the chefs (and their assistants) made over the course of the next hour. We personally loved the ingredients – they included things like squid, conger eel, and Chinese cabbage – foods that are far afield from our Western eating experiences.

After the chefs finished cooking, three celebrity guests, including film stars and food critics, would rate the dishes and a winner would be crowned.

To be honest, the winner never mattered to us. What mattered most was what the chefs did in the kitchen during their cooking time. Remember: these chefs had only one hour to create four to six dishes with an ingredient that was only JUST revealed to them. The dishes had to taste great, look beautiful on the plate, and have a well-balanced flavor profile.

Each Iron Chef had a small group of 2-3 assistants. The Iron Chef would quickly identify what the team would make, then set them off to work. Like a well-choreographed ballet, they would cut, chop, sear, bake – and constantly collaborate.

Every member of the team knew where they were going and what the others were working on. And, if something went wrong, they adjusted and changed course immediately **together**. Soufflé just fell? Quick, turn it into a sauce. Have a bunch of black ink you just took from the squid? Use it as an ingredient in the ice cream (yes, this actually happened). Burned the asparagus? Throw it in the blender with some peppers and make an asparagus salsa.

The important thing is that the team never stopped. They were constantly *improvising as a team* – changing and creating, creating and changing. And when they failed, they pivoted to something else without letting failure stop them. No one said, "I can't believe you just did that." It was more like, "OK, we just lost our third dish. What do we do?"

Can you think of other good examples of teams that improvise in a similar manner? How about any fast-action sports team, like basketball, hockey, and soccer? Each sport requires a team that has practiced and worked together over time, and it's usually fairly obvious which teams have practiced more when they get out on the playing field or court. Out there, the team might be trying to execute a structured play and has to respond and react to changing conditions all the time. Really great teams respond as if they are living and breathing as one.

Why does this matter? *With improvisational collaboration, you have to practice so that you're ready when it counts.* In a study at Stanford University's School of Business,

"...they found that the most innovative teams were the ones that spent less time in the planning stage and more time executing – instead of planning, they improvised. Contrary to what many managers believe, the more time a group spent planning in advance, the slower project development was."[11]

Why do you think that is? Well, the more you talk and plan and THINK about things, the more opportunity your brain has to engage that Judge. The more the Judge gets his hooks into the process, the more likely it is that he'll shut down new ideas.

In order to suppress this regular engagement of the Judge, you have to practice improvisational collaboration.

---

[11] Sawyer, K. (2007). Group Genius. In Improvising Innovation (p. 28). New York: Basic Books.

Section 3
The Four Rules of Improv

*In the long history of humankind (and animal kind, too)
those who learned to collaborate and improvise most
effectively have prevailed.*
                                        – Charles Darwin

I t's hard to believe we would need rules in improv – it
seems like an oxymoron. Things are just supposed to
happen, right? But, we do need rules. Think about it like
this: to yield the most consistent results and to get to the good
stuff of trusting and free-form creativity, we need a
framework – something that we can hang our hats on that all
of us can understand. Rules give our teams a common
language.

And, as we've been saying, we need to practice those rules
by doing exercises, just like a hockey player or an Iron Chef.

In this section we are going to explore how specific rules
are applied in the kind of improv practiced by *Whose Line Is
It Anyway?* and *Second City*. We will look at each rule in
detail and then discuss how these rules can be applied to the
world of business.

The four rules of improv are:

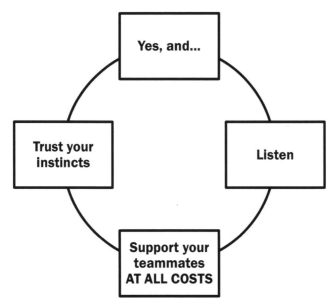

Figure 9: The Four Rules of Improv

They look really simple, don't they? They're not. We promise.

Rule 1: Yes, and...

How many times a day would you say that you utter the word "No?" 10 times? 20 times? 100? (If you're a parent, the number most likely increases exponentially!) Contrast that number with how many times you say the word "Yes." If you're anything like our clients, you'll find that the difference might be 10 to 1, or even 20 to 1.

We are exceptionally good at saying "No," both in life and business. The word "No" helps us protect our own skin. We practice saying it every day, over and over, in part because the Judge is constantly guiding us toward risk avoidance.

Let's look at a business example where NO played an important role: Blockbuster video. Remember the days of standing in line to rent a video? The days when Blockbuster would guarantee that they had the latest title out and charged absolutely outrageous late fees? (We're fairly sure we put a kid through college with those late fees.)

In 2000, Netflix CEO Reed Hasting hired a private plane, flew out to Blockbuster and pitched selling a 49% stake in Netflix in order to become Blockbuster's digital streaming service. They'd even take the name Blockbuster.com. At the time, Netflix only had 300,000 subscribers, and the bursting of the dot.com bubble was still fresh. Blockbuster famously said, "No."[12] Today Blockbuster is nearly out of business and Netflix is...well, a multi-billion dollar company and the first choice of many for streaming a movie online.

You might be saying to yourself, "Yeah, but that's just business. Blockbuster made a business decision with the information they had at the time. Good or bad."

And you might be right. It's easy to be an armchair quarterback and look back and say, "Well, they should have done X or Y." However, maybe, just maybe, if their executive team practiced the process of "Yes, and..." their brains may have been more prepared for thinking creatively, and they would have seen the opportunity in a far different light. It happens. We've seen it.

---

[12] Auletta, K. (2014, February 3). Outside the Box. Retrieved February 8, 2016, from http://www.newyorker.com/magazine/2014/02/03/outside-the-box-2.

Let's explore the other end of the spectrum. Let's look at a company that has "Yes, and..." tied to its corporate DNA: Pixar, Inc.

> *"The process of bringing the skills, ideas, and personality styles of an entire team to achieve a shared vision...is critical to the process of generating ideas and solving problems" at Pixar. '**Yes, and...' is part of Pixar's common lexicon that fosters creativity and keeps the vibe and energy in the room upbeat and alive.***"[13]

And it's no wonder (at least to us) that improv is integrated into the core curriculum at their Pixar University!

Looking at their box office receipts, you can see why this might be important. ***Pixar is tremendously profitable***. Their typical cost for a movie averages $96M, yet their Box Office receipts average $466M. ***$466M!***[14]

Not bad for a little animation company, right? We believe that everyone could use a little of that Pixar magic in their businesses, and one way to spark that magic is by focusing on the same thing Pixar does: "Yes, and...."

So, how does this "Yes, and..." thing work?

As we mentioned earlier, you're already great at saying "No." "Yes," on the other hand, takes work and discipline because it often requires you to take a risk and try something new (something that Blockbuster was unwilling to do).

The main concept of "Yes, and..." in improv works like this: You have to say "Yes" to anything that's given to you. It's that

---

[13] Capodagli, B., & Jackson, L. (2010). Collaboration in the Sandbox. In Innovate the Pixar Way (pp. 62-65). New York: McGraw Hill.

[14] the-numbers.com. (2015, January 20). Box Office History for Disney-Pixar Movies. (Nash Information Services, LLC) Retrieved February 8, 2016, from http://www.the-numbers.com/movies/production-company/Pixar.

simple. If someone is working through an exercise and says, "Check out this pineapple," you can't say, "No, that's not a pineapple. That's a baby." Or, if someone says, "Whew, it's so cold right now," you can't say, "No, it's hot." Instead, you have to acknowledge what the person just said with a "Yes," and then ADD to it with the "and...," which means you are adding to whatever was originally given.

For example, in response to "Check out this pineapple," you might say, "**_Yes_**, it's beautiful. **_And_** I'll bet you win the competition today." With this, you've accepted the pineapple AND added to the creation – a competition. Now your partner has a whole host of options to "Yes, and..." the competition aspect of the scene. Maybe they're worried about losing. Maybe they've grown the absolutely perfect pineapple. Maybe they're plotting their revenge against mean Mrs. Bates.

The response to "Whew, it's so cold right now," might be, "**_Yes_** it is, **_and_** I can't believe you brought us to Antarctica, Captain Shackleton." Again, you've said "Yes" and added to the scene by establishing who the person is and where you are.

The possibilities are endless as long as you say "**_Yes, and...._**" The possibilities stop as soon as you say "No." **_Creativity and innovation are all about possibility._** Saying "No" is all about control, and letting go of that control can be extremely difficult.

There are a couple of exercises that we like to use that can help get people into the habit of saying "Yes, and...."

The first exercise is called "*Yes, Point, Walk.*" With this exercise, groups of up to 15 people stand in a circle facing in, shoulder-to-shoulder. One person (we'll call him "Jack") points at another person ("Paige"). When Paige realizes she is being pointed at, she must make eye contact and say "Yes" back to Jack. Then, two things happen simultaneously. Jack (as soon as Paige has said, "Yes") begins walking to take Paige's location in the circle. Paige must now point at another person in the circle (Tom) and wait for Tom to say "Yes." This is important: Paige cannot move until Tom says "Yes" – even if Jack makes it all the way into Paige's space. This continues for several minutes until everyone in the circle has had a chance to move to different locations. Then, you can add a layer of difficulty by having everyone do the exercise silently – people only point without saying "Yes." And finally, you can do it without ever pointing, just eyes making contact.

This game ALWAYS stumps our participants. They get the order of things wrong. They say "Yes" when they point instead of when they are being pointed at. They get in a hurry and forget to say "Yes" to the one pointing at them. And the biggest error of them all, they start moving to the "new" spot before they have the acceptance from that person.

Though simple, this exercise can have very powerful results because the group is practicing saying "Yes" to anyone else in the circle.

Let's dig a little deeper into those errors. It's interesting that this exercise can be incredibly enlightening when it comes to your team's weaknesses.

The basic act of "accepting" the point from the other person seems to be the first struggle. The participant is often so busy thinking and preparing for the next part of the exercise that they have intellectually and physically moved on to the next step. In our experience, this is an indication of a lack of trust in the other person and/or in themselves, or a lack of understanding of the directive. Teams can fall victim to this when there is a goal set for them, and one or more of them rush to get started with the tasks BEFORE they have a comprehensive understanding of all of the guidelines or requirements. It's similar to when we were in school and there were those couple of students that rushed through the instructions to get to the test, completely missing that the correct way to title their page or fill out their name ended up counting for a large percentage of their grade.

Another mistake in this activity occurs when someone has accepted the "point," then senses the other person coming toward them and therefore feels compelled to move before they have connected to another team member with their own point and received a "Yes." The pressure of having someone moving toward them, ready to take their spot, is too much and they lose the objective of their next step(s). We liken this to the anxiety team members can feel when they are sometimes forced to "drop" a task in order to get something else done. The burden of knowing there's a deadline associated with their next task causes them to leave the other task incomplete.

With practice, this exercise teaches the basic process for saying "Yes" over and over. Think of it as a warmup for your daily workout.

E Another exercise for practicing "Yes, and..." is called "Look, I have a..." In this exercise, everyone pairs offs and stands face-to-face to their partner. One person (we'll call her Alice) starts by saying, "Look, I have a..." and then follows it with anything that comes to mind. And we mean *anything*. For example, she might say, "Look, I have a pirate ship." The second person (we'll call him Frank) responds back with "Yes, and...," and builds onto that original thought. For example, the second person might say, "Yes, and I can't wait to board her, Captain. I'll go get the oranges." Once the response is done, Frank then starts with his own "Look, I have a..." idea that is completely unrelated to the first "Yes, and...." So, Frank might then say, "Look, I have a washing machine that's broken." And Alice might respond with, "Yes, and it's your fault that we never have any clean clothes for the baby." This continues back and forth for several minutes.

The point of the exercise is two-fold. First, you have to say "Yes, and..." no matter how crazy the first idea is. Second, you have to build on the idea regardless of what is given to you.

Does this exercise apply in a business setting? Remember: coming up with new and innovative ideas requires you to think and act differently. You have to disrupt the natural cycle of the Judge in your brain, which is constantly moving you away from risk. With practice, saying "Yes, and..." moves you toward something new, something different, and something potentially risky.

It's fascinating to see how this concept of "Yes, and..." plays out with our clients. After a few gentle corrections to identify when someone has said "No," the team themselves always seem to begin self-policing. We've had administrative assistants call out CEOs when the "Yes, and..." rule has been violated.

Months later, we've had those same CEOs tell us that "Yes, and..." has been adopted as a standard meeting practice.

"No" and "Yes, but..."

Remember how we mentioned earlier in this section that people are naturally compelled to say "No?" The effects of the word itself can impact team dynamics in significant ways. Think about what happens when you're trying to build a team or perform a task. Having someone standing over you saying "No, that's not right," or "No, we shouldn't do it that way," has a negative effect. What would happen on a hockey team if every time the puck was passed to a specific player, that player refused the puck and knocked it back the other direction. And, yet, persistent use of the word "No" occurs in the corporate world all of the time. (Think of your last business meeting.)

Researchers at the Brookhaven National Laboratory conducted a study where they analyzed what happens in the brain when we hear and process a "No." Using fMRI, they found that when you process a "No," the regions in the brain that control anger light up. Additionally, your reaction time takes a nose dive – meaning that whatever you're doing at the time, it then takes you *longer to do* because you have to change gears to get your brain back into the task. So, every time you hear a "No," in that moment *you get slightly worse at the task you are doing.* [15] This is probably not that surprising to any of us, but understanding that there are real consequences at the neurological level continues to support the need to say "Yes, and...."

At this point you might be muttering to yourself, "But I just bought a book that teaches me how to say 'No' so that I can

[15] Alia-Klein, N., Goldstein, R. Z., Tomasi, D., Zhang, L., Fagin-Jones, S., Telangm, F., ... Volkow, N. D. (2007, August 7). What is in a Word? No versus Yes Differentially Engage the Lateral Orbitofrontal Cortex. Retrieved February 8, 2016, from www.ncbi.nlm.nih.gov/pmc/articles/PMC2443710/.

decrease my stress levels and increase my free time!" and here we are encouraging you to work on saying, "Yes, and...." Hang in there, we'll address how to use "Yes, and..." to soften a "No" in the next subsection.

If you step back and look at the prevalence of the word "No" within organizations or corporations, you can start to imagine its negative impact on corporate culture (we discuss culture in more detail in Section 4). At a fundamental level, "No" affects every person on every team within an organization, pulling down those creative employees that have the potential to innovate.

Here are two exercises that can help you and your team to notice the prevalence of the word "No."

 ### Count the number of times you say Yes/No in a day.

This exercise works best if you get your entire team to participate. Simply count the number of times you say "Yes" and "No" in a day. Try to be mindful of all of your conversations – texts, emails, face-to-face, etc. At the end of every day, document the numbers for the entire team. Do this for one week. We suspect that the numbers will surprise you. Later, after you've practiced Brain Disruption, perform the exercise again

and see if there is any difference in the Yes/No distribution. You will almost certainly see a levelling out of the two words as team members begin to see the often negative effects of saying "No," and get much better at saying "Yes."

Identify when people say "No" to you

This is a twist on the previous activity. Flip your awareness and track the number of times you **receive** the word "No." Make note of how many times you hear "No" from co-workers, family, friends, and other people in your everyday world. Can you identify any themes for why "No" was the response? Themes might include: time of day, how you are asking a question, and whether the question was asked with other people present or alone.

By the way, there is another way that we say "No" without being aware that we're saying it. The phrase "Yes, **but**..." essentially does the same thing as "No," it's just a bit more subtle.

- "I believe we can get this prototype to market by next quarter, but we can't sell it until June."

- "That was a great report, but the format is all wrong."

- "Yes, we could do what you're asking, but there's a big presentation coming up and no one has the time."

With "Yes, **and**..." and a simple tweak of the language, you can change these comments in a positive direction. For example, the last comment in the list above could be "Yes, we could do what you're asking, **_and_** we'd better adjust the time constraints."

As you're working through the last two exercises, consider adding "Yes, but..." to the overall counts of "No." And then make attempts to remove it from your everyday language.

One More Comment on Yes, and...

We often get a lot of skepticism about "Yes, and..." when we start our workshops. We recently worked with the executive team of a large hospital, and you wouldn't believe the amount of eye-rolling and comments like, "Yeah, you don't know our company." This can be a tough concept, in part because the Judge is fighting the concept itself.

Our point is that you need to open yourself up and get better at saying "Yes, and..." to things because you're already fantastic at saying "No." Remember, the possibilities are endless as long as you say, "Yes, and...."

Every once in a while someone will ask, "What if we **HAVE** to say "No" to something?" Well, then we believe that you should say "No" to it. Making a decision that will jeopardize your business? Yeah, say "No" to that. However, the point is to **get into a more consistent mindset of saying "Yes, and..." and see what changes**.

We also encourage the practice of saying "Yes, and..." even when you have to admit you can't do something. In some instances you may have to say "No" based on the timing of a specific request. For example, Mark has a huge deadline he is trying to meet and a co-worker asks him to help with another project. Here's how this situation could go down:

Sally: "Mark, could you give me some support on the Thompson proposal?"

Mark: "No, I have a deadline for Wayfair and I am committed until the end of the week."

Or,

Mark: "I'd love to BUT I am swamped with Wayfair."

What if the conversation went like this?

Sally: "Mark, could you give me some support on the Thompson proposal?"

Mark: "Yes, and I have some free time early next week. Will that work?"

Now, if that doesn't work for Sally, she still feels that Mark was willing to help – not that she's being denied. Yet, in a way, that's just what Mark did. He was honest in saying he could support her with the project and the timing was bad for him. Then, he gave her a realistic timeline for helping her.

Let's try another example – one of our clients, a multibillion dollar energy company, was trying to figure out a new way to standardize how to design and build production facilities. Their current model was based on uniquely designed facilities for each specific location. From a functionality standpoint the design was great – each design was perfect for its spot. However, from a scalability standpoint it took forever to execute because everything was custom designed. Vendors couldn't pre-design anything because they wouldn't know what to build. And for maintainability, it was very difficult for the field technicians because every site was different, from the equipment down to the nuts and bolts. Challenging, right?

The company brought in a diverse group of people from their organization to think through the problem – field techs, engineers, designers, and regulatory advisors. And they wanted us to help them.

One particular sticking point was around regulations. With so many legal constraints and permitting requirements surrounding energy companies, going fast seemed nearly impossible. There was no way to get "creative" around regulations and it became very easy to default to "No!" So what could be done?

By becoming aware of "Yes, and...," and practicing it diligently, the team was able to focus on specific limitations within the regulations themselves. They discovered together that there were ways to influence regulatory decisions and timing, which would help them dramatically increase their speed to market on certain projects. "Yes, and..." kept the possibilities open without getting caught up in "Well, it's a regulation, so there's nothing we can do."

Additionally, we guided them through several workshops focused on an analysis of current practices with regards to their designs. Through the use of "Yes, and...," they determined that a few modifications to the pre-fab engineering process would be less expensive than the customizations they'd been making to each location. They went from an attitude of "We've always done it this way," to answering questions like "What could be changed?" and "Is there another way?" This started a conversation that was so exciting that nearly every person in the room was on their feet with a dry erase marker in hand creating the new design.

Ultimately, they made such radical changes to their design that they estimated that they would **save more than ten million dollars in their first year of implementation.**

Rule 2: Listen

Listen

A lot has been written about listening and the importance of improving listening skills. Look through a *Harvard Business Review* or any issue of a leadership magazine and you'll probably find an article on listening. Most of what has been written is about active listening, which involves:

- Demonstrating that you're listening (nodding, saying, "uh huh" every once in a while)
- Clarifying points with questions
- Improving the physical environment (distractions, location)

But this isn't a book on active listening. It's a book that discusses the skills for **actually** listening, which is different from "active" listening, and a rarity in business today. In a recent survey, a group of corporate executives were asked to rate the most important skill for today's workforce, and 80% said it was listening. Many of those same executives said that listening was the area where most improvement was needed for their workforce.[16] We would argue that, despite widespread "active" listening, businesses continue to identify deficits in listening as one of their biggest concerns because people are not **actually** listening.

Listening in improv is a critical skill, and it's practiced in two ways: listening to your teammates and listening to yourself (which we will explore in Rule 4: Trust Your Instincts).

---

[16] Salopek, J. (1991, September 1). Is Anyone Listening? Training & Development.

Listening is an area that we find can be especially challenging for our clients. Just about every team we've worked with starts off not listening to each other well. At all. Why is that?

Because listening can be tough.

Let's look at it this way. When you're in a team you have great ideas. You just know that they're great. As soon as someone else is talking, however, you don't have a chance to articulate your ideas. Now it becomes battle – "Get my ideas out there before the other person does. Otherwise they'll ruin the flow."

Ever have that experience around a conference table? You're in a room with one, four, or ten other people trying to solve a problem and everyone is trying to speak. Because, after all, you are brilliant and have brilliant ideas.

Or, maybe you're on the other end of the spectrum. Maybe you feel that you simply can't speak because everyone else won't stop talking. Or that it isn't worth forcing your idea into the discussion because you can tell that people aren't really listening to each other.

The skill of listening in improv isn't about getting your ideas out OVER someone else's. It's about acknowledging input and creating something together with your partner or team. If you're in the driver's seat, and only in the driver's seat, you'll never get the perspective of what it's like to be a passenger. And sometimes (many times?) you'll need to be a passenger.

Here are some interesting facts about listening:

- 85% of what we know we have learned through listening

- Humans generally listen at a 25% comprehension rate

- In a typical business day, we spend 45% of our time listening, 30% of our time talking, 16% reading and 9% writing

- Less than 2% of all professionals have had formal education or learning to understand and improve listening skills and techniques (less than 2%!!!)[17]

There are a number of exercises that we use that are particularly good for encouraging listening. One exercise is called "The Five Second Rule."

EIn this exercise, two participants are asked to come to the front of the room. Let's call them John and Jenn. The group provides a suggestion for how to get a two person scene started. For example, a moderator might ask for an item that is typically stored in a hall closet. The answer could be a ski helmet. Now John and Jenn start a two person scene with "ski helmet" as their jumping off point.

The secret to the scene, however, is that neither of them can say anything without waiting for a full five seconds after the other player has spoken. The exercise might play out like this:

[17] W. Goodall, "Developing Healthy Relationships by Listening," 18 February 2015. [Online]. Available: http://www.northwestu.edu/watchmen/article/developing-healthy-relationships-by-listening/. [Accessed 8 February 2016].

John: Man, it's cold. I can't wait until we're on the slopes. I'll at least be able to work up a sweat.

Five seconds go by.

Jenn: I'm already sweating from that walk from the car.

Five seconds.

John: Well, you still look beautiful to me.

Five seconds.

Jenn: Wow. That's quite a compliment for a first date.

Five seconds.

John: Look, I thought skiing would be fun. Active, you know? Your online profile said you were outdoorsy.

Five seconds.

Jenn: I meant that I like to go outdoors. Sometimes. Not actually BE OUTDOORS DOING STUFF!

And so on.

This exercise is productive because it prevents the participants from piling ideas onto each other while at the same time giving space to each idea before moving on.

It also highlights those people who tend to railroad ideas. They, in particular, have a tough time adhering to the five second rule without opening their mouths.

We often use this exercise when we are conducting a brainstorming session. We start by having everyone stand in a circle, facing each other. We announce whatever problem we're working on, and ensure that everyone has a clear understanding of it. Then, the group takes turns either coming up with a new solution or responding to a solution that's been given to the circle, following the rule that **there must be five seconds before each response.** Also, everyone must participate at some point.

Here's an example from a customer service client of ours:

Moderator:	We need to improve client wait times on the phone without increasing our staffing.
	Five seconds.
Participant 1:	It seems like there are two approaches to me: technology and process. Or some combination of both.
	Five seconds.
Participant 2:	Yes, and process is most likely the cheapest of the two to fix.
	Five seconds.
Participant 3:	OK, so if we focus on process...What keeps our agents from resolving the call within the first two minutes?
	Five seconds.
Participant 1:	Training? Maybe they don't know how to answer?
	Five seconds.

Participant 4: Don't we have a huge database with lots of answers that they can search?

Five seconds.

Participant 5: I hate to ask it, but how complicated is it to search?

Five seconds.

Participant 2: I think it's OK, as long as you know what you're looking for.

Five seconds.

Participant 4: Has anyone in here actually used the tool?

Five seconds.

Participant 6: I have. It's tough.

The session went back and forth from there, and the team uncovered that the customer service search tool was particularly burdensome. Only a few employees knew how to use the tool effectively. The few who did were also the employees with the best response times. In addition, because the customer service reps were compensated for being in the top five for response times, the top performers were not motivated to teach their co-workers how to use the tool. The top performers could lose out on their bonuses!

By the end of the session, the team had worked out a plan to address training around the tool, identified ways to fix the bonus compensation, and assigned super users to work with I.T. to improve overall usage.

The Five Second Rule can be a very powerful tool because it requires people to stop jumping in, allows time for participants to hear and process what is being said, and encourages people who typically would not participate to speak up.

E Another tool we use to develop listening skills (and overcome listening challenges) is called Conducted Story. The exercise begins by identifying a group of four or five participants who come to the front of the room. They face the rest of the group while standing in a tight semi-circle, as if they are a small choir. The moderator is responsible for "conducting" the story. A participant may speak only when the "conductor" points at them, and must stop speaking immediately when the moderator stops pointing at them, whether it's mid-thought, mid-sentence, or even mid-syllable.

Once everyone is in place, the exercise begins with the conductor asking the rest of the group for a title to a story that has never been told before. Once identified, the title is then repeated by the four or five people standing at the front of the room. For example:

Conductor: May I have the title of a story that's never been told before?

Audience: The Hummingbird and the Moth.

Conductor: The Hummingbird and the Moth. Thank you. Choir, please repeat.

Entire Choir: The Hummingbird and the Moth.

The Conductor then points at one of the choir members. That choir member MUST speak and start telling the story of The Hummingbird and the Moth.

> **Choir 1:**   There once was a hummingbird that had a broken wing...

And so on from there. When the Conductor stops pointing, that person stops speaking. When the Conductor points at someone else, that person starts speaking and must continue the story right where the other person left off.

Now, this is one of those exercises that can really go anywhere – it totally depends on what the Choir comes up with. And there is NO WAY anyone can predict where the story might go.

The critical point, however, is that the Choir members **must** be listening to each other for the story to make sense.

This exercise is particularly good at identifying moments when people aren't listening. For example, here's someone who didn't listen to what came before.

> **Choir 1:**   There once was a hummingbird that had a broken wing. He was very sad that he'd broken his wing and was sitting on the edge of a...

The Conductor stops pointing, which forces Choir 1 to stop. The Conductor then points to Choir 2.

> **Choir 2:**   The moth hated the hummingbird.

You can see that Choir 2 didn't follow along and finish the sentence to "sitting on the edge of a...." Rather, they jumped to a completely different part of the story. If this happens, it's necessary to call out the behavior so that those listening skills can continue to be developed.

The point of both the Conducted Story and the Five Second Rule is this: You must ***practice listening to each other*** to ensure that you move the team forward. Each exercise has the ability to identify when members of a team are listening to one another and when they're not. Listening is something that we all assume that we do well, but the truth of the matter is that all of us could probably use the help.

Note that listening is closely intertwined with the rule "Yes, and...," because you can't say "Yes" to something if you didn't hear it in the first place!

Rule 3: Support Your Teammates
AT ALL COSTS

| Support your teammates AT ALL COSTS |

We like to teach that there is a life or death component to improv. Yes, we know this is an exaggeration. But, in improv, it's crucial to support your teammates with the commitment that you either fail or succeed ***together.*** There's no "individual" – you are all working to create something that you couldn't have created alone.

Let's look back at our Iron Chef example. If one member of the Iron Chef team makes a mistake by burning a giant sea scallop, it doesn't help anyone to stop and have a team meeting to analyze the mistake or why it's important not to make mistakes. Instead, team members gather, improvise a solution, change directions, and **MOVE ON.** (Yes, that happened, and...)

Something similar could be said of great basketball teams. If a play goes wrong, the team resets and gets ready for whatever comes next. There's no time to stop and discuss. Later on, in practice, they'll work on drills to prevent whatever went wrong the time before. But in the heat of the moment, they understand that mistakes are part of the game – maybe today will be your turn to make one, and tomorrow it might be someone else's turn.

Now, you might be thinking, "Well, come on, businesses are a little different. It's not a game or a reality TV show." But the importance of *supporting your teammates* should be just like the behavior of a great basketball team. You need to celebrate the good decisions, support the bad decisions, and move on.

Take a moment to think about the teams that you're on right now at work. Is there that kind of commitment and support? Do you, right now, support your teammates AT ALL COSTS? Do they provide that kind of support for you?

We'll bet not. The current corporate culture may encourage something more like, "I'm just trying not to get stabbed in the back," or "Team? What team?"

Do you remember the characteristics of a perfect team that we wrote down in Section 1? They included things like:

- Trust
- Know what the goal is
- Work together

- Communication
- No judgment
- Different backgrounds
- Everyone contributes
- Have fun

In our opinion, the most important characteristic is the first item on the list: trust. Trust is the core component of "Support your teammate AT ALL COSTS." In improv, when someone walks out and says there's a giant walrus right in front of you, they have to trust that you won't say, "I don't think so. It looks like a snail to me." They have to trust that you'll "Yes, and..." that walrus and move forward, and you have to trust that they'll do the same.

Trust is a tricky one, though, because we know at a fundamental level that trust is earned. But, **through the practice of improv**, you can run drills and get better, just like a basketball team or the Iron Chef.

E Let's look at an exercise: One Line at a Time. This is a quick exercise that is designed for 4-10 people. It requires a whiteboard and some different colored whiteboard pens. The goal of the exercise is to have the team draw an intricate image together, one line at a time.

To start the exercise, one person steps forward and draws a single line on the board. Then, a second person steps forward and adds a second line that supports the first line. A third person steps forward and adds a third line. And so on.

The exercise is complete when all team members agree that the image is finished, which most likely takes two or three cycles through the entire team.

As you might have guessed, this exercise is predicated on Rule 1: Yes, and.... Once a line is drawn it can't be erased. It's up to the next person to find a way to support and justify whatever was put up there.

Also, there's almost no way to control the direction of where the drawing is going to go. You have to accept that whatever was in your mind when you put your line up there will be totally different by the time it gets back to you.

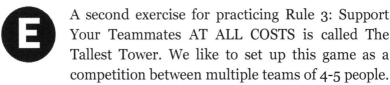 A second exercise for practicing Rule 3: Support Your Teammates AT ALL COSTS is called The Tallest Tower. We like to set up this game as a competition between multiple teams of 4-5 people. The goal is simple: the group that builds the tallest tower wins. And we offer the winners something of value – usually individual $10 gift cards to a nearby coffee chain. This helps raise the level of the competition because they are working toward something that they want to win.

We start out by giving each group the same materials. Typically, the materials consist of the list below, though you can improvise with whatever you might have available – as long as every team has the same items.

- A paperclip
- A straw (in wrapping)
- A binder clip
- Two sticky labels

- Two wooden coffee stirrers
- Chopsticks
- Two index cards

The teams have 10 minutes to build the tower. The tower must be freestanding and stay upright for 30 seconds once the 10 minutes are over.

And there's one more rule: For the first four minutes the team has to **discuss** their approach for building the tower **without touching the materials.**

This exercise can illustrate a number of things for the team. First, the competition aspect adds a layer of immediacy and stress, much like the Iron Chef. People can act differently (good or bad) when they are competing. Second, there will be team members that are more comfortable in the "discussion" portion (the first four minutes) than the "build" portion (the last six minutes), and vice versa. Third, the exercise will allow the competitors to use their newly-learned skills of improvisation. The materials will NOT work like they expect them to or have planned. They will have to **support** each other through determining a new solution.

In this activity, there's a great deal of information to gather. How long do we have? How will these materials respond once we get our hands on them? Do we know what all of these materials weigh? What are our roles? Will someone be the "builder" and others give advice? Has everyone given input? And on and on...

Then, once in the thick of building the tower, are you listening to one another? Are you supporting each other in saying "Yes, and...?" Are you able to be agile in your thinking of what you should do if what you originally intended isn't working? Are you exhibiting trust?

Rule 4: Trust Your Instincts

Trust your instincts

The last of our four rules, "Trust your instincts," is all about allowing yourself to trust the first idea that pops into your head. It's the consistent practice of tamping down the Judge and stepping out to take a risk and try something new or different.

Strangely, we find this flies in the face of the culture at most companies. Our entire lives we've most likely heard the phrase, "THINK before you SPEAK." And, honestly, that's a really important part of being a healthy functioning adult. It can save our lives! But, we're not talking about this in a setting where you need to be truly mindful about what comes out of your mouth. We're talking about using this rule when you innovate, brainstorm, and problem solve. Those are the times when you can't afford to think through and question every word like you would for a boardroom presentation. You can't allow that self-editing part of you to get in the way of creativity.

Researchers at a European University found that people have innate instincts when it comes to creativity, but as you get older you grow more likely to mistrust those instincts. Yet, these instincts are exceptional at solving problems. The study found that people who dare to investigate different ways of thinking and to be open to alternatives are more likely to actually solve something that's challenging.[18] So, the better

---

[18] Nelissen, J. M. (2013). Intuition and Problem Solving. Curr. and Teach., 28-2, 27-44.

you are at trusting those instincts, the better you will be at dealing with that next wall that's in front of you.

E One exercise that we use to practice trusting your instincts is called "First Word, Best Word." In this exercise a group of 5-10 people stands in a circle, facing in. Everyone starts clapping quietly or snapping to an established beat. Once the group is clapping/snapping in unison, one person states a single word in rhythm. The person on their left says a single word that relates to the word that was just said. Then everyone says the words together, followed by "Da-Duh-Da-Duh." The person who stated the last word begins with a new one, and this continues around the circle until everyone has had a chance to do it twice.

It looks like this:

Everyone begins snapping.

Person One (in time with the snapping): Pickle.

Person Two (in time with the snapping): Jar.

Everyone: Pickle-Jar. Da-Duh-Da-Duh.

Person Two: Standing.

Person Three: Tall.

Everyone: Standing-Tall. Da-Duh-Da-Duh.

Person Three: Skinny.

Person Four: Jeans.

Everyone: Skinny-Jeans. Da-Duh-Da-Duh.

Person Four: Pickle.

Person Five: Sky.

Everyone: Pickle Sky. Da-Duh-Da-Duh.

It's critical that participants don't overthink their responses. They just have to state whatever comes into their brains in the moment. There's NO time to prepare. If they think too much, they'll be off rhythm.

And the words don't necessarily have to be in context. It's completely acceptable as teams are working on this skill to see:

Person Four: Pickle.

Person Five: Sky.

Everyone: Pickle Sky. Da-Duh-Da-Duh.

The point is to ***keep it going.***

This exercise is ideal for setting up the foundation for brainstorming sessions. When you brainstorm you want people to have the freedom to say anything in response to something else. You want the ideas to flow. The rhythm and the speed of this exercise force people to listen and respond, without taking time to determine whether it's the "right" response.

We typically add one more layer to this exercise once everyone gets comfortable with it. We alter the rules so that the words CANNOT relate to one another. It might look like this:

Everyone begins snapping.

Person One: Tree.

Person Two: Pants.

Everyone: Tree-Pants. Da-Duh-Da-Duh.

The point is that the participants should be listening closely in order to respond in rhythm.

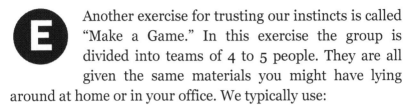 Another exercise for trusting our instincts is called "Make a Game." In this exercise the group is divided into teams of 4 to 5 people. They are all given the same materials you might have lying around at home or in your office. We typically use:

- 15 Lego® bricks of varying sizes and styles
- A deck of cards
- A pair of dice
- Chopsticks
- String
- Paperclips
- Post-Its®
- Pens
- Ketchup packets

The teams have 20 minutes to make up a game that they will demonstrate to the rest of the group. They have to use at least four of the materials, though they can use more if they want to. At the end, the game that is the most fun to play, as voted on by the rest of the groups, wins.

"Trust your instincts" comes into play as the teams begin their creative process. Invariably there are two types of teams: the team that **plans** and the team that **does**. Can you guess which team is typically the winner? The doers. The doers are the first to start throwing out ideas and trying things.

This is an important point: the teams that trust their instincts and get to DOING almost always win.

The Importance of the Rules

As you might have guessed, all of the rules of improv are closely intertwined. For example, if you're doing almost any of the exercises we listed above, it's impossible to say "Yes, and..." if you're not listening to what's being given. And it's difficult for you to trust your instincts if you're not getting support from the team or saying "Yes, and...."

So, why is the practice of these rules so important? Why do they matter?

In business, we have high expectations of our teams. We want them to get out there and solve problems, innovate, and make our companies more profitable.

We've found that teams that practice these rules shorten the time it takes to complete tasks, trust each other more, and listen better.

In the 1960's, Bruce Tuckman identified four stages of group development that every team goes through as they work towards completing any task. Those stages are: Forming, Storming, Norming, and Performing, and each stage is defined with specific characteristics (Figure 10).

Forming	Storming	Norming	Performing
• Team meets each other for the first time • Orientation • Establish ground rules • Polite • Members are treated as strangers	• Express opinions as individuals • Resist control • Infighting over leadership, definition and norms • Demotivation	• Accept others viewpoints • New roles are adopted • Personal opinions are expressed	• The group becomes capable • Flexible • Open • Supportive • Trusting • Solutions emerge

Figure 10: Tuckman's Stages of Team Development[19]

In today's fast paced business environment, we are moving on and off teams quickly. The practice of improv equips team members to accelerate through these various stages of group development by establishing a shared language and framework for developing trust, new ideas, and acceptance.

Think about it: Imagine if everyone in your company already knew and practiced the rules of "Yes, and…," Listen, Support your teammates AT ALL COSTS, and Trust your instincts?

By learning and practicing the rules of improv, the first three stages of Tuckman's model are compressed, allowing your teams to accelerate through to becoming higher performing teams faster.

Tuckman's model, then, looks like this (Figure 11):

[19] Tuckman, B. W. (1965). Development Sequence in Small Groups. Psychological Bulletin, 63(6), 384-399.

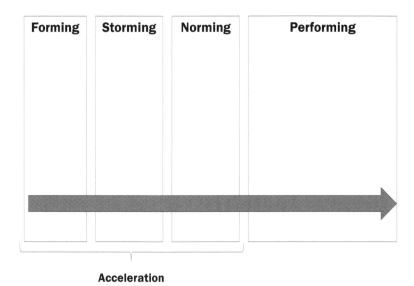

Figure 11: Tuckman's Model with Brain Disruption Acceleration

Remember those improvisational collaborators we discussed earlier? Let's look back at the hockey example. Imagine if every time you put a hockey team together, the team members had to learn (or re-learn) the rules of the game. They'd need to learn how to hold a hockey stick, what the "puck" is, and how to score a goal. It would be a nightmare.

Now imagine if the hockey team you're bringing together already understands how to play, can ice skate, and knows what happens during an "icing" penalty. The results of this team would be drastically different than the inexperienced team. We KNOW that.

But, why do we expect success from our business teams without equipping them with the rules of the game? Especially when we know that those rules would improve how they perform together?

Imagine if you could increase the speed at which you could get teams to the Performing stage by 10%. Or 25%. Or 50%.

Now *that* would have a giant impact on your business.

You can do that with ***Brain Disruption***.

Section 4
Culture

An organization's ability to learn, and translate that learning into action rapidly, is the ultimate competitive advantage.

– Jack Welch

Up to this point we've been discussing the brain and new ideas somewhat myopically by focusing only on you or your team. But, with Brain Disruption, we realize that there is something that can be far more powerful in either severely limiting or enabling innovation. Something that directly influences creative output and behavior: your corporate culture.

You can think of culture as the lifeblood of your organization. It represents everything you do right and everything you do wrong. It sometimes can seem like its own person – like a long-term employee who has incredible seniority, but who no one can remember why they were hired in the first place.

Corporate culture can be very difficult to pin down or define. Many of our clients can't even seem to agree on the *state* of their corporate culture. You can perform a survey with detailed questions about culture and get vastly different responses from everyone. And, not surprisingly, the executive team's perspective will often look nothing like the general employee response to questions like:

- Do you feel trusted?

- Does management encourage creativity?

- If you fail, is the response a celebration or a nail in your coffin?

- Is your company efficient at running meetings?

- Do you have a voice?

- Do people listen?

- Are your teams developed and supported by executive leadership?

- Are your company values just some words on a list, or are they deeply engrained into how you do things?

You must at least address or acknowledge the culture you have before you can create, repair, or build a new one.

For this reason, it's important to take a moment to dig a bit deeper into this whole concept of culture. We have a few clients who have done a culture analysis and brag about how "in tune" they are with their staff. Yet, when we work with them, we show them within the first hour that their culture analysis yielded nothing more than an awareness of larger issues. They never established a plan for managing critical gaps that were preventing them from functioning more efficiently or effectively. They never changed their culture.

What makes a culture tick? What's it really made of?

Think of your culture as a complicated patchwork of different factors that are all stitched together. We think of those factors as inputs that look like Figure 12.

Figure 12: Inputs to Culture

History: Your history is not only how your organization was founded, it's also the myths and legends that surround it.

How You Do Things: This represents how your company gets work done. Are managers expected to hold weekly status meetings? Do you use a project planning methodology? What technology do you use to enable collaboration?

Signs and Symbols: Signs and symbols exist throughout your organization. They include not only outwardly visible symbols (like your logo, or your Mission/Vision/Values statements), but also *signs of power*, like corporate jets or weekly cocktail gatherings.

Hierarchy: As you might expect, your hierarchy represents how you are structured to get things done. Who's in charge? Who reports to whom? Why is the reporting structure like it is? Most importantly, how does this affect the culture of the company?

Strategy and Financing: This represents things like budgeting, requests for money, and strategy definition and direction.

Decision Makers: The decision makers are not only those people who are higher up in the hierarchy, but can also include informal decision makers who other employees turn to when they need answers. For example, that executive secretary that holds the keys for who can see the CEO has informal power within the company.

A Culture of Innovation and Creativity

Where are innovation and creativity in all of this? In innovative companies, innovation and creativity influence everything, and vice versa (see Figure 13).

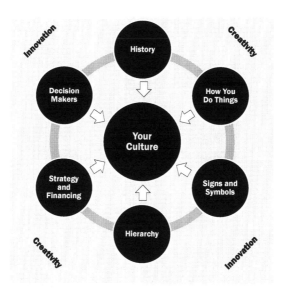

Figure 13: Inputs to Culture with Innovation and Creativity

 You probably have certain impressions of what the culture of a creative or innovative company would look like. Take a second and list the positive characteristics in the table below.

Positive Characteristics of Creative or Innovative Companies	
1)	9)
2)	10)
3)	11)
4)	12)
5)	13)
6)	14)

Positive Characteristics of Creative or Innovative Companies	
7)	15)
8)	16)

Figure 14: Positive Characteristics of
Creative or Innovative Companies

This is a tool that we often use in our workshops, and it always amazes us how **consistent** the results are. Are any of the characteristics listed below similar to yours?

Positive Characteristics of Innovative or Creative Companies	
1) Fun	9) Collaborative
2) People listen to new ideas	10) Like a start-up
3) Free food (yes, our clients actually say that)	11) Everybody is part of the team
4) High level of trust	12) Open floor plan
5) Open	13) No fear
6) Fast-paced	14) Positive working environment
7) Forward thinking	15) Passionate
8) Allowed to fail	16) Learn quickly

Figure 15: Positive Characteristics of Creative or
Innovative Companies (examples)

Notice anything similar to the Four Rules of Improv we discussed in Section 3? Hint: Listening and Trust. There are also two other concepts that are closely related – Fun and Failure, both of which we'll explore a little later in this section.

Not surprisingly, many successful companies weave the words and concepts around "Fun," "Trust," "Listening," and "Failure" into their core values, which helps to influence their corporate culture. Below are a few examples (Figure 16).

Company	*Published Core Values*
CarMax	Fun Communication Teamwork Respect
DaVita	Fun – We enjoy what we do. We know kidney dialysis is hard work; but even hard work can be fun. We take our jobs seriously, but we feel a fun environment delivers better care to our patients while creating a better work environment for our teammates. We strive for excellence and we have fun. Team – One for All, and All for One! We work together, sharing a common purpose, a common culture and common goals. We genuinely care for and support, not only those to whom we provide care, but those with

Company	Published Core Values
	whom we work shoulder-to-shoulder. We work together to pursue achieving our Mission.
Zappos	Create Fun and a Little Weirdness Embrace and Drive Change Build Open and Honest Relationships With Communication Build a Positive Team and Family Spirit
Netflix	Curiosity (learn rapidly; seek to understand; broad knowledge) Innovation (re-conceptualize issues to discover practical solutions; challenge prevailing assumptions; create new ideas that prove useful) Courage (say what you think; make tough decisions; take smart risks; question actions inconsistent with their values)
Southwest Airlines	Fun-LUVing Attitude: • Have FUN • Don't take yourself too seriously • Maintain perspective (balance) • Celebrate successes

Company	Published Core Values
	• Enjoy your work • Be a passionate team player
The Motley Fool	Collaborate: Do great things together. Innovate: Search for a better solution. Then top it! Fun: Revel in your work.

Figure 16: Corporate Core Values (examples)

Let's be honest, though – A culture of innovation and creativity is more than a series of 10 Core Values posters or a plastic wallet card affixed to your security badge (though that's a start). It's a language and a behavior. You have to:

- Define it
- Teach it
- Practice it
- Reward it

T Let's find out a little bit about YOUR corporate culture. The questionnaire on the next page is a useful tool for identifying how prepared your organization is for creative thought and innovation.

Statement	Rank (1 = Low, 5 = High)
1) Your people have the skills they need to be creative in their work.	1 2 3 4 5
2) Your processes are helpful to new ideas.	1 2 3 4 5
3) Your processes encourage creative problem-solving.	1 2 3 4 5
4) Managers do not take new ideas away from people who care most about them.	1 2 3 4 5
5) There are reward mechanisms for failure.	1 2 3 4 5
6) It's easy to get people together to solve a problem.	1 2 3 4 5
7) Failure is accepted.	1 2 3 4 5
8) People do not waste or disrespect new ideas.	1 2 3 4 5
9) Diversity of people is	1 2 3 4 5

Statement	Rank (1 = Low, 5 = High)
encouraged.	
10) Corporate politics do not get in the way of a good idea.	1 2 3 4 5
11) New ideas are not treated harshly when they are shared.	1 2 3 4 5
12) Failure is encouraged.	1 2 3 4 5
13) There are reward mechanisms for new ideas.	1 2 3 4 5
14) You trust the people you work with.	1 2 3 4 5
15) When you have a new idea, you know where and how to share it.	1 2 3 4 5
16) Your people stand behind decisions once they have been made.	1 2 3 4 5

Figure 17: Innovator Questionnaire[20]

Now go ahead and score the results. Take the corresponding value from your answers above and plug them into the Figure 18.

[20] McKeown, M. (2014). The Innovator's Toolkit. In The Innovation Book (pp. 52-242). Harlowe, England: Pearson.

Creative People		*Processes for Creativity*	
Question	Scoring	Question	Scoring
1)		2)	
4)		3)	
6)		5)	
8)		7)	
9)		10)	
11)		12)	
14)		13)	
16)		15)	
Total		*Total*	

Figure 18: Innovator Questionnaire Scoring

This is a questionnaire that we'll use with clients who are looking to build a culture of innovation. The tool can be extremely useful because it quickly gives you a barometer of where you, your team, or your company are with regards to innovation and creativity.

Regardless of the size of the organization, we'll typically start by conducting 15-20 interviews with mid- and upper-level leaders, using this tool as the conversation starter. The results can be quite enlightening (and for senior leaders quite terrifying).

Take your results from above and plot them on our Innovation Lifecycle Matrix in Figure 19.

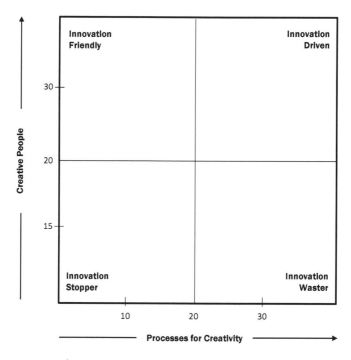

Figure 19: Innovation Lifecycle Matrix

Where did you end up?

Innovation Stopper: Your organization does not want or accept new ideas. New ideas are frowned upon in deference to the idea that "This is how we've always done it." Failure is never tolerated.

Innovation Waster: Your organization is interested in new ideas, but corporate politics come into play every time there is a whisper of change. People are more interested in protecting themselves and their ideas than the company. As a result, only the people with the greatest political influence get a new idea pushed through.

Innovation Friendly: Your organization has creative people who have great ideas, but no formal method for collecting and nurturing those ideas, let alone applying them. There are few incentives for getting out there and trying something new. Therefore, unless someone has an idea that is a guaranteed win, ideas sit and wallow.

Innovation Driven: Your organization has a framework for identifying and developing new ideas. Anyone can share an idea up and down the political corporate chain and is rewarded for doing so. If the new idea fails, people do not place blame. Rather, they learn from the failure and move on to the next big innovation.

As you might imagine, our clients rarely end up in the Innovation Driven category. At an organizational level, we find that most organizations trend into the Innovation Stopper category.

But what can you do about it? Honestly, we've found that it really depends on your organization. There is not a single prescription that applies to all companies, and it's important that the approach is tailored for your specific challenges, hierarchy, and organizational design. That said, there are some high-level issues that can be addressed for each category (see the table below).

Lifecycle Category	*Potential Questions*
Innovation Stopper	With Innovation Stoppers, the first two things to address are: failure and trust. If you really want a culture of innovation,

Lifecycle Category	Potential Questions
	people must be allowed to fail. This means that you need to spend time defining what failure really means and how you can begin to embrace it more. You must also identify why there are trust issues to begin with. Ask questions like: What happens when someone fails? How can we change the actions that get taken when people fail? What methods can we use to rebuild trust? Why are there trust issues?
Innovation Waster	The hierarchy of an organization is often the culprit for Innovation Wasters. Often, you must first fix how the organization rewards and compensates new ideas. Ask questions like: What prevents people from bringing up ideas if they have them? What are the political barriers that keep the organization from exposing new ideas? Is there training that could provide people with new methods for collaboration?
Innovation Friendly	Organizations that are Innovation Friendly often require a more formal framework for how ideas get bubbled up to the surface. Ask questions like: What rewards are available for people who think of new ideas? Is there a budget devoted to innovation? If so, how is it spent? If not, is there a way to make

Lifecycle Category	*Potential Questions*
	one?
Innovation Driven	Keep building upon what you're doing. Ask questions like: What's working and what isn't working? Is there additional training we can leverage? What else can we do to get people to think differently?

Figure 20: Questions for the Innovation Lifecycle Roles

Not only can the Innovation Questionnaire be used to document current cultural impressions of your employees, it can also illuminate powerful disconnects between different levels of the organization.

For example, Figure 21 contains the combined results of two teams from one of our clients, a large software development company. The two teams were the Executive team (5 members) and the Software Development business unit (15 members).

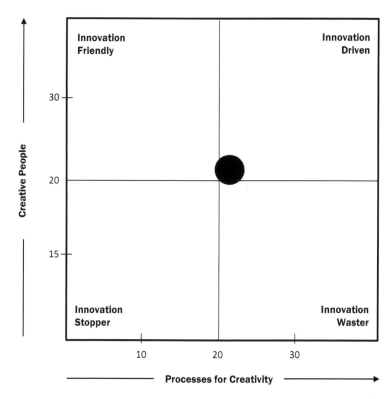

Figure 21: Innovation Lifecycle Matrix - Software
Development Company

Doesn't look too bad, right? They've just crested the edge of the Innovation Driven quadrant, and though they have room to grow, they're on the right path.

Now let's separate the results (see Figure 22).

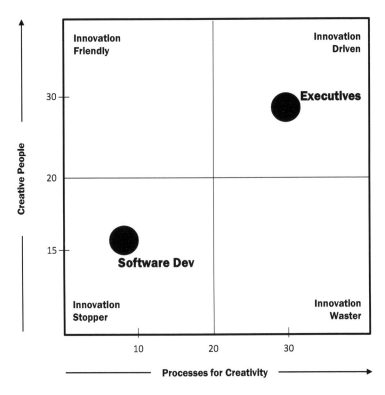

Figure 22: Innovation Lifecycle Matrix - Software
Development Company (cont.)

Now there seems to be a different story. As we continued to work with this client, we found out that the Executive team was certain that their company was very progressive with new ideas. But, the Software Development team – the team actually implementing the work – did not feel the same. Further analysis uncovered that there were a couple of members of the Executive team who were exhibiting behavior that significantly undermined trust. Once these individuals started working through their trust issues, the Software Development team felt more inclined to participate.

Interesting stuff that was easily identified through the use of the tool.

Our experience with this tool begs the question, why do most organizations seem to trend toward Innovation Stoppers? There can be lots of reasons, but we believe our experience suggests that it comes down to two things:

- Most businesses don't want to deal with new ideas. They say they do, but they don't. They have no formal way to recognize or reward a new idea, and most people are comfortable doing exactly what they always do – the same old thing. Why? Because change hurts. Better to ignore change than accept it (this is due, in part, to the Judge).

- No one is allowed to fail. If you fail, you're fired. Or something close to it.

What else can you do about it?

Our answer at a very basic level: ***Improv***.

All of the activities we've explored in this book, and many more we use with our clients, are steeped in the rules of Yes, and..., Listen, Support your teammate AT ALL COSTS, and Trust your instincts. As we've hoped you've learned, improv allows you to practice these rules at a very rapid pace while adjusting the architecture of your brain to be more responsive and more flexible. Additionally, improv allows you to ***practice failure,*** over and over and over again.

And in improv we do something else with failure – we celebrate it.

Let's Celebrate the Thing
We Hate Most: Failure

When was the last time you celebrated a failure at work? We're talking about the kind of failure where someone has a great idea and tries to implement it. And then it falls flat, or breaks something, or explodes! Our bet: it's never celebrated. Instead, we couch "failure" into meetings like "post-mortems" and "lessons learned." "How can we make sure that we never do this again?" we ask ourselves. But we don't **celebrate** it. It's a failure. And businesses hate failure.

Well, that's just ridiculous. And we want you to think so, too.

Let's start with a simple example – imagine you are a toddler learning how to walk. How many times do you think you will fall as you learn? A hundred times? A thousand times? Think about how useful it would be to sit down and have a meeting every time it happened, being told that it could "never happen again," or that you needed to describe and document the lessons you've learned.

Come on. That would be a horrible way to learn. And we hope that, in reality, most parents will just stand off to the side and laugh and clap and encourage you to try again. They are motivated to encourage you because it's a big deal!

If you want a culture of innovation and creativity, failure has to be treated as something that is AWESOME.

By design, **improv gives you a way to practice failing**. Don't know how to do a Scottish accent? Well, you were just told that you're a Scottish shepherd, so step out there and be brave. You'll fail miserably, and we'll celebrate by laughing. By practicing failing through improv, we've found that you're better equipped to deal with "big" failure, and more likely to accept the risk of failing.

Have you ever seen the movie "Groundhog Day" with Bill Murray? It's a movie about a selfish, arrogant weatherman who is suddenly living the same day over and over again. After utilizing those days to his benefit and engaging in all sorts of crazy behavior, he begins to realize there may be a reason he is stuck in a "time loop." There is a scene toward the beginning of each day that the character relives where he steps in an icy pothole in the street. He does this several days in a row until one day, just as he is about to step in it, he stops, lifts his leg and steps OVER the hole. He learned from his previous "failure"!

If Edison's lab had a culture of reprimanding every failure, do you think he would have invented the lightbulb? What about the 39 failures before the invention of WD-40? Or how about the 5,721 prototypes before Dyson completed his first cyclonic vacuum cleaner? That's not a made up number, by the way. 5,721 prototypes!

Celebrate failure – and in doing so you celebrate the effort of trying something new, which provides fertile ground for innovation.

"But, how can you ***actually celebrate it?***" you might be asking.

There are several companies that have begun to spotlight their failures in fantastic ways. The company NerdWallet, for example, has a "Fail Wall" full of Post-it® notes bearing the failures of everyone, including the CEO. We believe that there's something refreshing about that. Actually seeing that you are not alone in your failure, or that everyone fails no matter what their level, creates a diving board from which all employees can jump.

Tor Myhren, an ad agency executive, designed a Superbowl campaign for the Cadillac Escalade in the mid-2000's. It was such a colossal failure that it won several "Worst of" awards. This failure, however, did not keep him away from the world's largest advertising audience. The following year he created the E*Trade baby ad, which had a successful multi-year run. You may remember the ad campaign – it featured a baby seated at a computer. The baby would talk directly to the camera about how he was trading stocks on E*Trade. He'd say things like, "Boom! I just bought some stock." It was a tremendous, multi-year success.

To help foster new ideas, Myhren started the "Heroic Failure Award," which he presents each year to the employee with the most epic fail. They get their name engraved on it, too![21]

The Indian company Tata Innovista has created the Dare to Try awards, which are given out for the best failures. The organization has a team that analyzes overall effort and potential impact, focusing on "what was learned from each failure" as the important component. The winners are recognized directly by the CEO in front of the entire company.[22]

At the end of the day, we learn by failing. If your employees aren't rewarded in some way for the crazy and "almost" ideas they bring to the table, ***then why would they ever keep***

[21] Moran, G. (2014, April 4). http://www.fastcompany.com/3028594/bottom-line/a-real-life-mad-man-on-fighting-fear-for-greater-creativity. Retrieved February 8, 2016, from http://www.fastcompany.com/3028594/bottom-line/a-real-life-mad-man-on-fighting-fear-for-greater-creativity.

[22] Sundheim, D. (2013, January 9). To Increase Innovation, Take the Sting Out of Failure. Retrieved February 8, 2016, from https://hbr.org/2013/01/to-increase-innovation-take-th/.

doing it? In fact, most of their ideas are probably not even making it to a second thought because they keep remembering what happened to that intern that decided they had a great idea and sent a memo to everyone – and then was never seen again. Finding time to weave this concept of celebrating failure into the very core of who you are as a business is key if you want to be truly innovative.

However you celebrate failure in your organization, make sure it's BIG. You don't need a huge budget to do it, either. You just need to mark the occasion somehow, and make it matter.

Is Anybody LISTENING?

Communication is essential to a healthy corporate culture. What kind of communication is exhibited in your teams? Do they text more than email? Do they email more than call? Do they call more than visit face-to-face? All of these methods of communication are important and have their place. Just remember that there is a "best" communication method for each situation, and your teams need to pick the right ones.

We have a good friend who consulted as a language translator for online information sharing. She told us that no one was allowed to communicate with one another in person. They were expected to Skype or use instant messenger, and that was it. She talked about how painful it was to be unable to get up and go to someone to ask a question or clarify something.

We're certain that the decision to be "technology-only" for communication was a rational one (most likely driven by cost). However, in our experience we've found that the absence of face-to-face time often leads to a lack of understanding and assumptions, and a deterioration of relationships between parties.

MIT's Human Dynamics Laboratory recently released a study in which they were able to predict the success of a team by analyzing the team's communication patterns. They didn't analyze **what** the teams said to each other within the team, but rather **how** they said what they said.

The researchers started with a group of call center agents and had them all wear electronic badges around their necks that recorded their physical interactions with coworkers, including things like: what direction they were facing, how long they spoke, and whether they nodded or used hand gestures. Based on the data, the researchers could then predict that Team A, for example, would be more successful at a particular task because their communications – both formal (in meetings) and informal (chatting around the water cooler) – involved engaged interactions that had a balance between talking and listening among team members. Again, the researchers didn't focus on the content of the conversation. Instead, they focused on some 100 different data points collected by each badge every minute.

The science behind this study is fascinating. From an evolutionary perspective, language is a relatively new process for the human brain. Underlying our verbal communication is a whole host of subtle cues that occur physically on an unconscious level – within our body language.

If we can understand the physical nature of a good team, then we can begin making changes that will have a significant improvement on our team performance. And the financial gains from altering how teams interact can be staggering. One company is predicting a $15M increase in productivity due to increased efficiencies in team interactions.

So, at a high level, teams that perform well have members who:

- Talk to one another

- Are engaged when listening and have energetic gestures

- Listen almost the same amount as they talk

- Connect with the entire team, not just the person in charge[23]

Communication has often been seen as a "soft science," and yet it is anything but soft if we can increase profits by 15 million dollars through better team communication.

It's critical that we find mechanisms that change and improve team interactions at their very core. We need mechanisms that improve listening and trust, and focus on team results. Mechanisms like *improv.*

Know When to Lead, Know When to Follow.

Over the last several decades there has been a focus on Leadership within organizations and companies (and we mean Leadership with a capital "L"). What we find is that, on the whole, our clients have countless practices for teaching employees how to lead. "Good leadership is so important," they'll tell us. And we don't disagree, for the most part. In our workshops we'll witness leaders who are really good at

[23] Pentland, A. (2012). The New Science of Building Great Teams. Harvard Business Review (April 2012).

leading...or, at least, taking charge. If we ask a leader ,to improv, it might be nerve-wracking for someone to step out and start an exercise with an idea from the moderator of "dirty socks," but most of the members of an executive team seem to have no problem doing it. They lead things. Every day. That's their job.

Well, leading is only half the battle (actually considerably less than half, if you consider the statistic in the next sentence). You must have followers to lead, especially when "leaders contribute on the average no more than 20% to the success of most organizations." 20%![24] Therefore, we believe the more important topic lies in how organizations can breed cultures that encourage intuitive and talented **followers**. Improv is one of the few disciplines where everyone who participates has a chance both **to lead and to follow**, sometimes within seconds of each other (remember the core principle of "Yes, and..."). And you must practice doing both.

As we've come to find out, the follower/leader dynamic is directly related to trust. Think about it – it's almost impossible to really follow someone whom you don't trust to provide meaningful goals and productive direction. You might go through the motions, but in the back of your mind you're thinking, "This person doesn't know what he/she is doing." Additionally, it's impossible to lead effectively if you don't trust the people whom you're leading to follow through on your ideas.

MBA and executive training programs throughout the world emphasize the importance of leadership. Walk through the Business section of a book store and you'll see hundreds of books on it. We think there's been enough written about

---

[24] Kelley, R. E. (1992). The Power of Followership: How to create leaders people want to follow and followers who lead themselves. New York: Currency/Doubleday.

leadership. But what about the other side of the coin? What about *follower*ship?

Coined by Robert Kelley in the early 1990's, followership is a fairly easy concept to grasp. It's "the ability to take direction well, to get in line behind a program, to be part of a team and to deliver on what is expected of you."[25] If you expound on the concepts of "Yes, and..." and "Support your teammate at ALL costs," you begin to see how the rules of improv relate to making people **not only better leaders** in the context of decision-making and creative thought, **but also better followers** in terms of taking that thought and moving an idea forward.

Leadership and followership are reciprocally related, yet we spend most of our time worried about *how we lead*, even though most (if not all) of us are in a role where we report to someone else. If you move up the entire leadership chain within an organization, you'll find that even the leadership team most likely reports to a board. Everyone has to follow, at some point or another, and following can be very difficult.

So, let's ask a question:

What kind of follower are you?

Answer the questions on the next page and we'll find out. *(Important note: This is a fairly comprehensive survey of 22 questions. We know it seems a little long, but it's necessary in order to get the meaningful results.)*

---

[25] McCallum, J. S. (2013, September 1). Followership: The Other Side of Leadership. Retrieved February 8, 2016, from http://iveybusinessjournal.com/topics/leadership/followership-the-other-side-of-leadership#.VNZVdy5WJUl.

Question	Rank (1 = Low, 5 = High)
1) Although I stay quiet, I often question the reasoning for a decision, rather than just doing what I'm told.	1 2 3 4 5
2) I am enthusiastic. And that enthusiasm has a positive impact on my team.	1 2 3 4 5
3) I am quickly successful on new jobs or tasks by defining and meeting metrics that are important to the leader.	1 2 3 4 5
4) I believe in the company's goals and priorities.	1 2 3 4 5
5) I can be successful in completing task assignments that don't have a lot of definition or are ambiguous.	1 2 3 4 5
6) I can clearly articulate what I do well and what I don't do well.	1 2 3 4 5
7) I do whatever it takes to get the job done, even if I don't own it.	1 2 3 4 5
8) I enjoy playing the devil's advocate with my team and my leader.	1 2 3 4 5
9) I follow my own ethical standards over my company's.	1 2 3 4 5
10) I give my best ideas and highest performance.	1 2 3 4 5

Question	Rank (1 = Low, 5 = High)				
11) I go above and beyond.	1	2	3	4	5
12) I identify and champion ideas that will impact the company.	1	2	3	4	5
13) I like to make my teammates look good, even without getting any credit.	1	2	3	4	5
14) I set priorities and decide what's most important to achieve my team's goals.	1	2	3	4	5
15) I speak my mind on important issues, even though it might cause conflict with the team or with my leader.	1	2	3	4	5
16) I take the initiative to solve tough problems within the company.	1	2	3	4	5
17) I understand what is expected of me from my leader.	1	2	3	4	5
18) I work to become more valuable to the company by increasing my competence in mission-critical activities.	1	2	3	4	5
19) If someone asks me to change, I am more likely to say "Yes" rather than "No."	1	2	3	4	5
20) My job is either professionally or personally fulfilling.	1	2	3	4	5

Question	Rank (1 = Low, 5 = High)
21) Once a decision is made, I stand behind it 100% (even though I may have disagreed with the idea).	1 2 3 4 5
22) I get excited by learning new things.	1 2 3 4 5

Figure 23: Adapted from R.E. Kelley's Followership Survey[26]

Score your results in the table below by taking the corresponding value from your answers above and plugging them in.

Scoring:

Thinking On Your Own		Engaged in the Organization	
Question	Scoring	Question	Scoring
1.		2.	
6.		3.	
8.		4.	
9.		5.	
12.		7.	
14.		10.	

Thinking On Your Own		Engaged in the Organization	
15.		11.	
16.		13.	
19.		17.	
20.		18.	
22.		21.	
Total		Total	

Figure 24: Followership Survey Scoring

Take the totals and plug them in the 4x4 box in Figure 25.

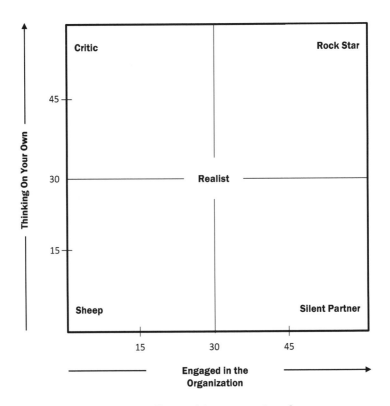

Figure 25: Followership Survey Graph

Where'd you end up?

Rock Star: The Rock Star is the person you want on your team or the person you want to be. They provide value and self-management, and they can see how they fit into the overall picture of the organization. They adapt quickly and efficiently and have a personal motivation to be good at their job.

- *What you should do if you're a Rock Star:* If you're a Rock Star – Congratulations! But, don't get complacent. Keep challenging the status quo, learning new things, and identifying methods to make you and the company better. Look for training opportunities to learn the latest in your field. Develop content and speak at a conference.

- *What you should do if you have Rock Stars on your team:* The biggest challenge with Rock Stars is that they can get bored easily. Continue to keep them engaged by involving them in decision-making and encouraging them to bring new ideas to the table. Send them to training on new technologies and new methods of doing things.

Critic: The Critic does a good job thinking of new ideas, but is much more comfortable criticizing the ideas of others than coming up with any of their own. They feel alienated, like no one understands them, and they revert to "the old ways are better" when a new idea comes up that is not theirs. As a result, they play the most dangerous role in an organization.

- *What you should do if you're a Critic:* Ask yourself: "Why?" There can be lots of reasons – baggage from a layoff, bad experiences with current leadership, not getting recognized when you felt you should have been, or just plain old fear of change. Document your reasons. Next ask yourself "What behavior would need to be exhibited for me to trust those around me?" *(probably many of the behaviors described in this book).* Then, begin engaging in activities that encourage others to demonstrate those behaviors. You have to start by addressing trust first. But, what if it's your boss you don't trust? Ah, that's a lot more complicated, but can start with something simple: Talk to them. See if you can find common ground and work from there.

- *What you should do if you have Critics on your team:* Focus on trust. Critics typically want to participate but they don't feel that they can for fear of reprisal. Without first finding ways to build a framework for trust, critics will never become Rock Stars. And regardless of what you do, they will most likely fight any attempt to move them. Just keep providing proof that trust matters. Follow through on your commitments and demonstrate the behavior you expect.

Sheep: The Sheep is the person who is neither engaged nor participating. They require a leader for everything. Think of the Sheep like the production line factory workers of the early 1900's. They are disinterested in establishing direction or providing input to new ideas.

- *What you should do if you're a Sheep:* You'll need a major overhaul of how you approach new thoughts for you to move towards being a Rock Star. Start finding ways to think and talk about new ideas, such as a weekly lunch or coffee where you ask people what else you could be doing. Come up with a new idea and run it by your boss. Find any way to participate in the decisions being made around you.

- *What you should do if you have Sheep on your team:* You're going to need a big change to your culture if you want to move Sheep into different categories. Start by identifying the culture that you want and involve the Sheep from the very beginning. Set expectations for behavior and follow through. Provide training on new idea development and trust.

Silent Partner: The Silent Partner is a person who is invested and engaged, but likely has no opportunity to express those thoughts. They rely completely on the leadership to make decisions and come up with ideas; otherwise they're comfortable keeping their head down and doing their job.

What you should do if you're a Silent Partner: It's great that you trust the leaders to lead and make all of the decisions, but that sure sounds boring! *(And we know that you have good ideas that you're keeping under wraps.)* Read books on best practices for your industry or function. Start an "idea lounge" where you talk about challenges with your peers. Start a book club and ask your leaders to participate. Go to conferences.

What you should do if you have Silent Partners on your team: Silent Partners need to be encouraged to imagine a new process or future. Ask your people what motivates them, then design incentives for new ideas that speak to those motivations. Provide training. Create an innovation space (see Innovation Room later in the section). Encourage employees to devote part of their work day to expanding their horizons.

Realist: Ah, the most common role. The Realist doesn't want to rock the boat. They are pragmatic. They might often utter the phrases, "I've seen this before," or "What's in it for me?" They have good ideas, but don't feel safe in bringing them up, preferring to stay quiet and follow the direction of others. They are engaged in the organization to a point, but prefer to keep their mouths shut and not make any drastic changes. They're like prairie dogs – constantly raising their heads up above the ground, then pulling them right back down.

- *What you should do if you're a Realist:* You really can go any direction, but you're on the fence. You need proof that new ideas matter, and the trust that they won't be shot down if you bring them up. Trust is an issue, as is your personal experience. You have to find ways to disrupt your current way of thinking at the same time as developing trust (like, oh we don't know...improv?). Read through the approaches for the Critic and the Silent Partner for ideas.

- *What you should do if you have Realists on your team:* The Realists are like the Sheep, except with more motivation. You need to involve Realists at the inception of any discussion about innovation, and then document every success and every failure. Trust us, Realists know when something works and something doesn't. Provide training and methods for deepening trust. Incentivize new ideas (see Incentives later in this section).

We often use this tool as part of a large-scale culture analysis to help gauge the temperature of a team or organization. First, it's useful to get an understanding about how **you** are "showing up," even though you may already be aware that you don't support the organization, or that you have new ideas but don't feel safe bringing them up.

Second, if you anonymously survey an entire group and plot the results, you get a sense of what you're up against with regards to implementing an innovative culture. Sure, you may inherently know which person is engaged and which is not, but this can be a powerful visual aid to illustrate the challenges you might face. And you may end up with some results that surprise you!

See Figure 26 for the results from one of our clients.

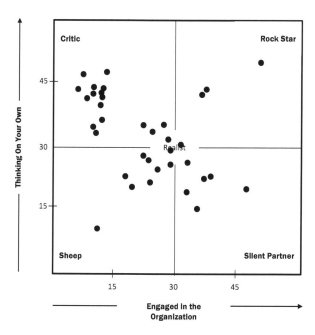

Figure 26: Followership Survey Graph (example)

Notice any problems? How about that cluster of Critics? These are people who know in their bones that they have good ideas, but they have a deep-seeded mistrust for the organization. Problem? Absolutely – but now you know that you need to address trust issues swiftly.

Remember: Knowing how to lead is critical to your organization. Knowing how you and your people *follow* is critical to an organization's success.

There's another vital reason for understanding followership: people who have higher followership scores have better job performance and higher job satisfaction. A recent study out of Northcentral University analyzed 131 employees of an automotive engineering and manufacturing plant. As part of the study, the employees were asked to complete a survey similar to the one you just did. Additionally, each manager was asked to rate the performance of the employees. The study found that the people who were in the Rock Star quadrant performed better and were happier employees.[27] So, if you increase your followership scores, you will most likely see increased job performance and satisfaction.

But how and why does the leadership/followership dynamic fit into improv? What's the relationship? Recall what we mentioned in the beginning of this section: you are required to both lead and follow in improv, sometimes within a matter of seconds. And you practice both.

Just like endlessly cutting onions as an Iron Chef or passing the puck back and forth in hockey, improv is a method for practicing leading and following in the same exercise, which makes you more prepared for when you actually have to do it in the real world. (Oh, and you work on trust and creativity at the same time).

---

[27] Favara Jr., L. (2009, April 1). Examining Followership Styles and Their Relationship with Job Satisfaction and Performance. Retrieved February 8, 2016, from http://pqdtopen.proquest.com/doc/305167384.html?FMT=ABS.

How does improv prepare participants for leadership AND followership? Well, there are three "roles," if you will, in improv: the Initiator, the Reactor, and the Back Foot. Each role is an important component of an improv exercise.

- The **Initiator** is the brave soul who steps out with an idea. They are the ones who commit to making a choice and going with it, no matter what.

- The **Reactor** is the teammate who comes in almost immediately to support whatever (and we mean *whatever*) the Initiator has decided to do. Remember the rule: Support Your Teammate AT ALL COSTS.

- The **Back Foot** is any other team member who is listening for whatever support might be required.

Here's an improv example. Let's say that two women, Lisa and Elena, are on stage getting ready to play a two person scene. The moderator asks for an idea to get them started (in improv we call this a "give" and is part of the unpredictability of improv – you never know what you're going to get). The audience screams out a bunch of ideas and the moderator chooses the idea "bus stop." So, the idea, or the "give," for the exercise is "bus stop." That's all Lisa and Elena get. They now have to incorporate "bus stop" into the exercise.

The **Initiator** is the first person motivated who steps out to start the exercise. In this case, let's imagine that Lisa steps forward and starts nervously looking up and down the street, saying "I can't believe it's late. My boss is going to kill me." After several seconds or two she screams, "C'mon. Where is that bus?!"

Realizing that the scene now needs a bus (and doing a little "Yes, and...") the **Reactor** (Elena) immediately steps off to the side and pretends to be a bus driver driving a bus. She pulls up, stops the bus, and says, "Sorry I'm late. I hit a parked car, but nobody saw me."

As you might expect, the exercise can go anywhere from there.

Where does the **Back Foot** fit in and who does it? People who play the Back Foot are there to provide anything the exercise requires, without taking away from or detracting from the exercise. In this case, a couple of Back Feet might step forward and pretend to be other people at the bus stop, or people on the bus itself. They add character and depth to the exercise. They are there to support the team.

It looks like this (see Figure 27):

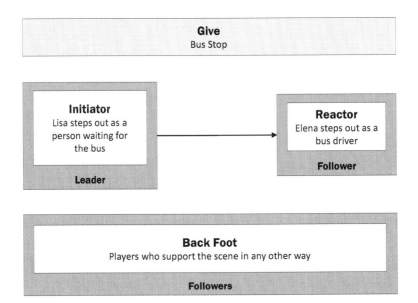

Figure 27: The Roles of Improv Layout

Personality Assessments

 Influencing your corporate culture takes hard work and discipline. It also takes people...who can occasionally be unpredictable. So it stands to reason that the more information you can gather about your people, the better.

Enter the Personality Assessment (PA). The PA is another great way to give you and your teams a common vocabulary, and to identify preferred and non-preferred methods of communication. It always makes us chuckle a little when we suggest doing this with our clients. The consistent gut response seems to be "umm...I did the Myers Briggs when I got married, why take something like that again?"

Our questions:

- When was the last time you used it?

- Do you make good use of the assessment in how you relate to your co-workers?

It's good to know the natural personality preferences of you and your team, and teams are more successful when they have team members who are self-aware.

There are lots of assessments out there (Myers Briggs, Insights, Hermann Brain Dominance, etc.). We like the **DISC Assessment** because it's been around for many years, is widely available, and has lots of information written about it. The DISC Assessment was created by Dr. William Marston, whose research determined that your choice or preference for behavior could be plotted into four quadrants. Each of those quadrants has associated personality descriptions (see the image on the next page).

More importantly, you can map those quadrants to the roles in improv (Initiator, Reactor, Back Foot). Why does that matter? Remember in the first section we discussed brain plasticity and making your brain more flexible? This is done not only by trying new things, but also by trying things that make you (and your brain) uncomfortable – like brushing your teeth with your non-dominant hand. We use the DISC Assessment to identify where people tend to be more comfortable in improv, then design exercises that force them into uncomfortable places (Figure 28).

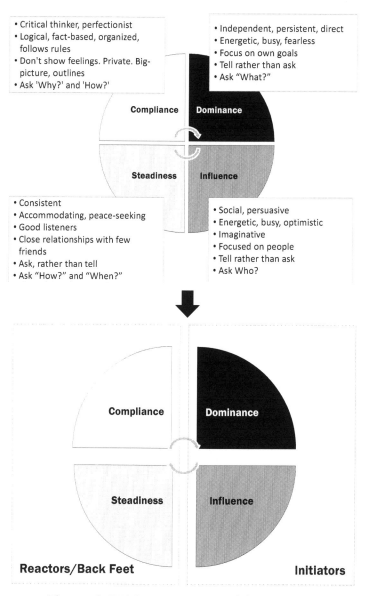

- Critical thinker, perfectionist
- Logical, fact-based, organized, follows rules
- Don't show feelings. Private. Big-picture, outlines
- Ask 'Why?' and 'How?'

- Independent, persistent, direct
- Energetic, busy, fearless
- Focus on own goals
- Tell rather than ask
- Ask "What?"

Compliance   **Dominance**

Steadiness   **Influence**

- Consistent
- Accommodating, peace-seeking
- Good listeners
- Close relationships with few friends
- Ask, rather than tell
- Ask "How?" and "When?"

- Social, persuasive
- Energetic, busy, optimistic
- Imaginative
- Focused on people
- Tell rather than ask
- Ask Who?

Compliance   **Dominance**

Steadiness   **Influence**

Reactors/Back Feet   **Initiators**

Figure 28: DISC Assessment Model Compared to the Roles of Improv

For example, in our experience, psychiatrists and IT Engineers seem to fall into the Compliance category, whereas Marketers identify with Dominance and Influence. By continually pushing teams out of their comfort zone and putting them in positions to work within the opposite side of their personality preference, the brain begins to make new connections and ultimately encourages new behaviors.

One caveat about Personality Assessments – they are not the final word. We've seen organizations that take so much stock in them that all they've done is given themselves another way to label each other. "Oh, you're an 'Influencer' and I'm a 'Compliant' – therefore I despise you." Or, "You're a 'Dominant,' therefore you're just going to walk all over me."

There's a continuum. As William Blake once said, "Everything in moderation. Even moderation."

Your People Don't Trust Your Company (by default)

Be ready – no matter what change your company is trying to implement, your people aren't going to trust it. This seems pretty obvious, right? In a recent study at Baylor University, subjects were analyzed using an fMRI and they found that:

> *"...during the scan, research subjects read short vignettes. Some were about objects, such as a piece of fruit or ironing board, while other stories told of people or corporations performing pro-social actions (e.g., donating to charity), anti-social actions (e.g., lying or breaking the law), or neutral actions (e.g., buying a printer)."*[28]

[28] Guittierez, G. (2014, November 17). Are Corporations People Too? Retrieved February 8, 2016, from https://www.bcm.edu/news/neuroscience/are-corporations-people-too.

As one might expect, specific areas of the brain became active when participants were asked about objects vs. people. However, somewhat shockingly, the areas of social reasoning that activated during questions about people *also engaged when asked about companies*.

What does this mean? It means that we interact with companies *as if they are human beings*. They aren't the static, monolithic institutions that we write about in business magazines. According to our brains, they are living, breathing entities, and this means that they are more likely to protect and keep what has worked in the past rather than adopting new approaches.

There's likely a component in evolution as to why we think this way: businesses haven't been around that long. Our brain is dealing with them the best way it knows how.

Also, companies have one more thing against them – our brain is negatively biased toward their actions. Through the study the researchers found that the brain is telling us that we should be suspicious of the actions of a company just like we should be suspicious of a stranger on a dark street.[29] RIGHT OUT OF THE GATE!

We all know that humans fear change. Add a layer of suspicion onto any change a business wants to make and things get more difficult. The new buzzwords of the 21st century businesses – innovation, creativity, flexibility – all require change on a very basic level.

---

[29] M Plitt, R. S. (2015). Are corporations people too? The neural correlates of moral judgments about companies and individuals. Social Neuroscience, 10(1).

So, how do you make people better at change? You practice it. You practice it in a safe environment where there are clear rules and expectations of behavior. You improv.

The Innovation Contract

Creating a culture of innovation and creativity takes work and commitment. We often have clients who call us and ask, "Well, can't you just get this done in a couple of days? Or a week?" Our answer: Absolutely not.

But, how do you get started in an effort to change organizational culture?

First, you need rules – rules that define how you expect the people in your organization to behave. A contract, if you will. But where should you start? Remember the Four Rules of Improv from Section 3? Start with those.

But you shouldn't stop there. We strongly recommend crafting a total of 10 rules that define this new innovative behavior (the number 10 has always seemed to resonate with our clients). Here's an example from one of our clients:

The Innovation Contract

1) Say "Yes, and…" before saying "No"

2) Balance listening with speaking.

3) Trust your instincts.

4) Fail. And do it quickly.

5) Support your teammates (at all costs!).

6) Start meetings on time. End meetings on time.

7) Value diversity of opinions and skills.

8) If you hit a roadblock with the team, stop and laugh. Then try again.

9) Get behind decisions, even if you initially disagreed with them.

10) Fun above all.

Don't spend hours crafting and rewording. Keep it simple so that everyone can understand it.

Next, make sure everyone understands the rules of the contract. You can't just march out and say "Here's how we're going to behave going forward" without giving context for why you're changing, why it's important, and what the expectations are. Once people understand "why" it's important, then it's much easier to get them to support the idea. You have to start by getting your entire team or organization behind the rules (and this can take a lot of work).

As we mentioned earlier in this section, your teams will be immediately skeptical of anything new that your organization is trying – their brains are going to fight it. Additionally, they might remember what changes came down the pipeline before, and how things "fizzled out" or lost momentum in the past. So don't underestimate the challenge of trying to move everyone into a single direction.

You will also need to determine what's going to happen when someone breaches the contract – holding people accountable is critical. Otherwise, people will just continue their same old behavior. One approach that a client of ours uses is to give their employees permission to state (or "call out") when someone isn't behaving according to the contract. Anyone along the leadership chain, from administrative assistant to CEO, can call out without reprisal. This behavior takes a tremendous amount of trust. But cultural changes won't stick unless the entire team or entire organization can get in on the act.

For example, one COO took the "Start meetings on time. End meetings on time" from the Innovation Contract to the extreme. If you didn't start within two minutes of the starting time, followed by clearly stating an agenda, other people were required to get up and leave. She then made a powerful step toward correcting behavior by testing it herself. She called a meeting with 20 or so employees. After five minutes of just sitting there and staring at her phone she stated, "I've violated our contract. I haven't started the meeting, nor have I said what we're going to do. And you're still here. This meeting is over."

 Other client approaches to change culture have included:

- Everyone at the table yells "No" when someone says "No." "No" offenders quickly become aware of when they are not supporting the "Yes, and..." principle.

- Require every meeting to begin with a fun activity. Each participant is required to laugh before the meeting starts.

- Use the 5-Second Rule (see Section 3) as a meeting facilitation approach. No matter what is said, no one can respond without first waiting 5 seconds (or any number of seconds you define).

- Party jar. If someone breaks a rule they are required to add $1 to a jar. At the end of the month, the company doubles the amount of money in the jar and throws a party (this way, both the organization and the person is on the hook).

Lastly, everyone needs to be reminded of the Innovation Contract. Place it in meeting rooms. Put it up on people's doors. Make it a visible and physical representation of your culture.

The Idea Pipeline

As you begin to tap into the collective knowledge of your employees and work to create a culture of innovation, new ideas will (hopefully) start coming your way. What's the best way to reward those ideas? How can you make sure that you keep them coming, and keep them coming consistently?

There's actually been a lot of debate over the last few years – should you give one giant prize like Google or 3M? A big payoff should motivate your employees, right? Or, maybe it's better if you give small prizes. Will that mean that your employees won't be as interested, though?

A recent study from the University of Southern Denmark analyzed both the big and small prize approaches. Interestingly, they found that big rewards can have a negative impact. Think about it like this – you're going to give, say, $100,000 to the team that comes up with the best way to solve what we'll call "Problem X." This presents a challenge – when you have a big reward, many people will want to solve it. So you'll get a LOT of solutions.

"But, isn't that the point?" you might be asking yourself. Actually, no. The researchers found that you'll most likely end up with an idea pipeline bottleneck. There will be many good, even great, ideas among the glut of submissions, but you'll have so many that you won't be able to go through them in a timely fashion.

According to the study, a better approach is to focus on smaller rewards, such as 5-15% of an idea's value. This in turn allows for a more consistent idea pipeline because not everyone and their dog are trying to get the big reward.[30]

By the way, this may seem to fly in the face of some of the earlier talk of "more ideas = more ideas of value." It doesn't. What we are talking about here is the INCENTIVE piece that drives your employees to submit those ideas. If you set the prize too high, folks have an instant need to submit every idea to "win." At that point, innovation becomes about "winning" and not about solving problems. Subtle though it might be, it is still an important distinction.

Regardless of the approach, one thing is clear: people need time to think about BIG innovations. You can't expect your employees to fit innovative thought and research into their day without making room for it. Many of our clients are under the impression that "OK, you've learned about innovation...now go and innovate," without adjusting workloads to allow for it. We cannot stress this enough: If you want people to be inspired to think differently, you need to give them time (and money) to do so.

There are many examples of forward-thinking companies (including Google, 3M, and Arrow) that allow their employees

[30] Baumann, O., & Stieglitz, N. (2014). Rewarding Value-Creating Ideas in Organizations: The Power of Low-Powered Incentives. Strategic Management Journal, 35(3), 358-375.

to devote 15-20% of their time to a project they want to work on. Menlo Innovations plans for every employee to have a 32-hour work week, with the remaining 8 hours devoted to training, exploration, and idea generation.

Remember: if you're going to change your culture, you have to commit to a new way of doing things. This includes *changing how your employees are spending their time* in order to make room for innovative thought. You can start by scaling back on low-value meetings and status reports. Come on – we know that you have them.

You also need to identify your feedback mechanisms for collecting new ideas. Look at things like:

- Employee suggestion box.

- Idea management software (though you have to address process first and not just expect that the technology will be your "solution.")

- Hackathons – bring all of your business analysts and programmers together to solve a specific problem. Spend one or two days (all day and all night) programming a solution.

- Innovation days – bring everyone together to solve a specific problem. Reward the solution.

Finally...FUN and LAUGHTER!

As promised, we want to end this section with some thoughts on FUN.

Two of the most important byproducts of improv are fun and laughter, and they really go hand-in-hand with each other. If you're having fun, you're most likely laughing, and vice versa.

The good news is that **laughing makes you feel good** – not just your state of mind, laughing actually **improves the physical state of your body**. There have been a number of studies over the last 15 years that have found that laughing:

- Provides a 27% increase in beta-endorphins, the body's natural pain killer
- Lowers cortisol, a stress-related hormone
- Dilates the blood vessels to increase blood flow
- Increases immune system antibodies[31]

In our experience, laughter and fun in the workplace are far less common than they should be. Yet, many people inherently understand that there is a relationship between laughter and a good place to work (Figure 29).

---

[31] R. Buck, "The Funny Business of Laughter," 30 April 2008. [Online]. Available: http://www.sciencefocus.com/feature/psychology/funny-business-laughter. [Accessed 8 February 2016].

Figure 29: Impact of a Fun Working Environment

Why don't companies do more about this? We find many of our clients *know* that fun and laughter are important, but there seems to be a prevailing belief that it's just not appropriate. As if there's a connotation to laughter that you're goofing off, and work is ***SERIOUS*** business. But, lately, cutting-edge science and research is proving that laughter is a critical part of team success.

At its core, laughter is largely about relationships. Think about the number of times you are alone in front of the TV and the number of times you laugh while you're sitting there. Now compare that to when you are in a social situation. You will laugh 30 times more in a group than you will by yourself![32] It makes sense, then, that there's a deep *social* context to laughter – you engage in it more when you are in a group.

So, how does this apply to teams at work? Researchers at the University of Amsterdam recently completed a two-year study that analyzed the relationship between humor in teams and their associated performance. What they found was something that we've been preaching since we started our company – the teams that laugh together *stay* together

The researchers recorded and analyzed 54 teams (352 people) over the course of the two years. First, they found that teams using humor laugh regularly together and **produce more and have better outcomes**. Second, they determined that laughter was a powerful way of setting up a creative task, and subsequently the teams that laughed together while they were brainstorming had *more* ideas.[33] That's exciting stuff!

We've had a similar experience with our clients. We commonly use the Alternate Uses Test (remember the Paperclip Test in Section 1?) as a method of measuring idea generation before and after our workshops. At the end of our workshops we've seen an increase across teas as high as 81%,

---

[32] R. Buck, "The Funny Business of Laughter," 30 April 2008. [Online]. Available: http://www.sciencefocus.com/feature/psychology/funny-business-laughter. [Accessed 8 February 2016].

[33] N. Lehmann-Willenbrock and J. A. Allen, "How Fun Are Your Meetings? Investigating the Relationship Between Humor Patterns in Team Interactions and Team Performance," *Journal of Applied Psychology,* vol. 99, no. 6, pp. 1278-1287, 2014.

with some individuals having as high as a 200% increase! We know that some of this is related to Brain Disruption – and along with that disruption comes laughter and fun.

Improv gives you a mechanism for engaging teams with fun and laughter by just learning how to do improv and then practicing it.

Section 5
The Brain Disruption
4i Methodology

*I can't understand why people are frightened of new
ideas. I'm frightened of the old ones.*
                                        – John Cage

The last part we're going to explore is the Brain
Disruption 4i Methodology. If you think of the structure
of this book as a pyramid, we've been focusing on each
concept in order, starting with your brain (see Figure
30).

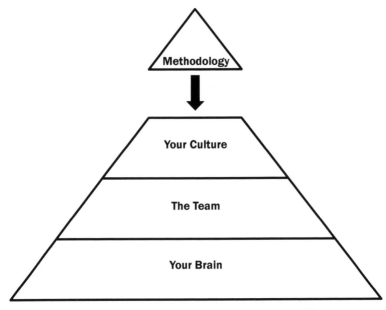

Figure 30: The Brain Disruption Pyramid

It's not a bad idea to think about the Brain Disruption process in this order. Only after you've addressed your brain, your team, and organizational culture should you layer on a formal innovation methodology for people to follow.

In our experience, however, organizations do just the opposite – they put methodology at the bottom of the pyramid and promptly ignore the rest of the levels, **expecting that the methodology will fix everything**. This approach has challenges. If you want the methodology to stick, you must begin by addressing core behaviors– because if you don't, you'll have a great methodology with lots of pretty tools and no one using them.

This doesn't mean that you can't introduce a methodology for innovation early on. As a matter of fact, having an innovation methodology can help a newly formed team prioritize a goal. Just do it AFTER you've introduced and practiced rules like: Listen, Yes, and..., Support your teammates AT ALL COSTS, and Trust your instincts.

Having studied various innovation methodologies that have come out over the last 50 years (from 1950's Osborn and Parnes creative problem-solving to TRIZ to OODA Loops to Design Thinking), we find that they all have similar structure.

Through our research and practical experience, we've developed the Brain Disruption 4i Innovation Methodology. It looks like this.

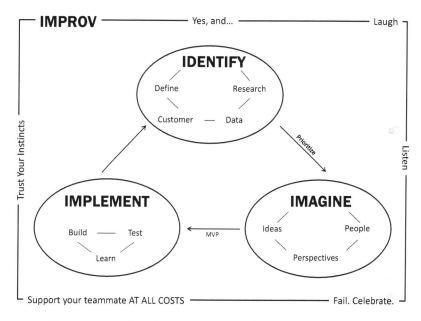

Figure 31: Brain Disruption 4i Innovation Methodology

Let's briefly explore each stage of the methodology and how each piece fits into the overall process.

Improv

You'll notice right away that IMPROV is the overarching or foundational stage in this methodology. You can't expect people to come together and begin working as a team without first giving them a chance to BE a team. And yet, most teams do this every day. Think about the last meeting you were in. Did you warm up the brain? Did you laugh? Or did you just sit around the table listening to someone talk?

We suspect we know the answer.

Improv gives teams the rules and vocabulary that set the framework for working and creating together – rules a-nd vocabulary that have to be practiced and studied (just like a basketball or hockey team). Improv puts you and your teams into the mindset to be radical, disruptive, creative, and it forces your team to focus on the core RULES:

- Yes, and...
- Listen
- Support your teammate AT ALL COSTS
- Trust your instincts

As well as:

- Laugh
- Fail. Celebrate.

Identify

The next stage is to IDENTIFY the problem or challenge you want to work on. You may already know what it is. You may not. Regardless, the steps are the same.

First, identify the question or problem you want to focus on. The question can be broad or specific, depending on your goals. Here are some examples from our clients:

- Why are we getting complaints with our new software?

- Why does IT have a bad reputation in the organization?

- How can we increase sales without adding headcount?

- What are the challenges of communication between our doctors and the staff?

- How can we provide consistent power throughout the design process?

Or, you can have a completely different goal and ask the question: "What's our next big invention?"

Second, bring a group together offsite and *research* the reasons why a problem is occurring. Use sticky notes and have team members write every reason why a problem could be happening. There's a change management part to this particular step – one goal is to get everyone on board with the problem, and another goal is to make sure people agree it should be solved.

Third, go and gather **data** about your problem or challenge. Gather data any way you can. Talk to your employees. Talk to your **customers**. Run focus groups. Send out surveys. Do hardcore research. Leverage feedback mechanisms with technology, like email, text, and website analytics. The sky is wide open as to how you want to do it. Just get data.

Most important: Have a conversation with (whether it be through technology or face-to-face) and listen to whomever you're defining as your "customer." Really listen.

Fourth, clearly **define** the problem based on your data and the information from the customer. If you don't have it right, start over.

> *Note: we often get asked the question from our clients, "You said offsite. Does the meeting really have to be?" The answer is no, but you need a space that is devoted to being creative – a creative suite, if you will. If you're onsite at your company, people are easily distracted and pulled into conversations. Get away. We promise it will help put people into a different state of mind. Or, spend money on that Innovation Room from Section 4.*

Imagine

The third stage in the methodology is to IMAGINE your solution. Bring your **people** together. Do Brain Disruption exercises, improv and start playing.

Diversify your team in order to get different **perspectives**. Look for people who are involved in the process of creation at all levels. Look for people who aren't involved in the process, but have good ideas.

This may come as a surprise to you, but most of us surround ourselves with people who think JUST LIKE US. This is called "Confirmation Bias." Think about your friends for a second – we guarantee that most of them think like you do. They agree with your perceptions of things, take the same side in discussions of difficult or polarizing topics, and generally "feel" the way you do about the world. This makes a lot of sense. Why would you surround yourself with conflicting views every day? This would make for a stressful life, yes?

With Confirmation Bias, the more we can surround ourselves with people who think and feel like us, the more we validate our own thinking and beliefs – and that feels good. We are mindful about justifying our views and opinions and actively seek out that support.[34]

It's not just your friends, though – you'll see this in business, as well. Bosses very often hire "in their image," making for a homogenous and consistent team. Great for the status quo...but what happens when you need to think differently?

One of our clients has chosen to deal with the Confirmation Bias by changing their hiring practices. If a candidate makes it all the way to the end of the interview process (which involves several rounds of interviews) and does not get a final selection by the team, a certain percentage of the rejects is actually

[34] Cooper, B. B. (September 13, 2013). Retrieved from https://blog.bufferapp.com/thinking-mistakes-8-common-mistakes-in-how-we-think-and-how-to-avoid-them. [Accessed 8 February 2016]

offered the job. The concept being that there are good reasons that the candidate made it all the way to the end, and that there's a high likelihood that Confirmation Bias is coming into play.

You don't need to take team diversification to such an extreme, however. As you're identifying team members for the IMAGINE stage, challenge yourself to look for people who are different from you. They might be in various parts of the organization, or in roles that are completely unrelated to the task. It doesn't matter what level they are – if they are good thinkers, they'll work.

 Once you have **people** and **perspectives** in place, come up with crazy **ideas** on how to solve your problem or challenge. Explore and evaluate your solutions. Talk about them. Play with them.

Once you're done, take all of your solutions, put a weight to them, and pick the ones with the most excitement and value. Rank them using the worksheet in Figure 32.

Instructions for the Idea Prioritization Worksheet:

1) Weight each question based on its importance (1 being the lowest, 10 the highest).

2) Rate the solution against the question (again 1 being the lowest, 10 the highest).

3) Multiply the Weight x Rating to "score" the idea on that particular question.

4) In the case of questions 7-10, the scores are "negative" because the idea may have a large impact on

the organization, or there is already a solution that could work.

5) Add up the values in the Score column to get the total score.

Question	Weight (1-10)	Idea #1		Idea #2	
		Rating (1-10)	Score (Weight x Rating)	Rating (1-10)	Score (Weight x Rating
Does the idea get people excited?					
Does the idea contribute value?					
Does the opportunity outweigh the cost?					
How feasible is the idea?					
Is there a way to build a working model without designing the entire thing?					
Does the idea solve everything it needs to?					
Is there a substitute for the idea?			-		-
Can we "buy" the idea? Is there something off-the-shelf that already exists?			-		-
Will we need new infrastructure to support the idea?			-		-
Are there far reaching impacts into other parts of the organization?			-		-
TOTAL					

Figure 32: Idea Prioritization Worksheet

Once you have your total scores, you should have a good sense of which idea might make the most sense to implement. Also, don't be limited by the ten questions we listed above. You might include additional questions that are unique for your organization. For example, if your company is international, there may be a language barrier or another infrastructure question to consider.

Implement

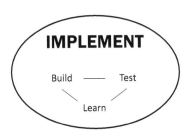

The fourth stage in the methodology is to IMPLEMENT. **Build** something quickly and get it out into the hands of your customer. ***IT DOESN'T HAVE TO BE A COMPLETELY FINISHED PRODUCT.***

Don't make the mistake of thinking you need to have everything perfectly designed before you release it.

Just **build** something – anything – with which you can gather feedback. Consider creating things like:

- A picture
- A comic strip
- A cardboard prototype
- A video or movie
- A fake front-end website
- A manual process that emulates all steps

- A role play

Do it. Then go and **test** your solution. Fail and **learn** everything you can. Document that learning and have it influence your design or idea. Then **build** it again.

This part of the process is based around the concept of a minimum viable product (MVP), popularized by Eric Ries in *The Lean Startup*. With this approach, you only develop what is necessary to test your solution, and see whether it's workable. Therefore, you limit your overall risk while still getting the valuable data you need.

There are lots of examples where the MVP- approach has worked well. For example, the founders of Zappos, the online shoe company, purchased shoes as they needed them from local retailers, rather than investing in their own inventory. This allowed them to test their business model without investing in additional overhead. The CEO of Dropbox, the online data storage company, created a video that demonstrated how the product would work, without an actual working product. He posted it to HackerNews and overnight they went from 5,000 to 75,000 people on their beta list. The user community went nuts. Flickr, the online photo sharing company, was conceived on a napkin.

The important thing is to get something out into the world so that you can see what works and what doesn't.

Time Boxing

There is one concept to keep in mind as you're working through any one of the pieces of the Brain Disruption 4i Innovation process.

How many times have you been in a meeting that spawns four additional meetings because people cannot make a decision? There can be lots of reasons for this – the right people aren't around the table, you don't have all of the information, or you have to reach consensus.

We find that there's a reason that's a lot more common: people are afraid to make a decision. Making a decision means that something will most likely change, and we've talked throughout this book about how the brain reacts to change.

Or, people get caught in the "Analysis/Paralysis Cycle," where it's more important to get just a little more information so that the best decision can be made...and then they require a little more information...and then a little more. And then NOTHING GETS DECIDED! We hate that.

We address this challenge through improv by "time boxing" – that is, setting a goal that a decision will be made by a certain time.

All improv exercises have a beginning, a middle, and an end. You know when they start, and you know when they're finished. During that time, you are forced to make decisions that move the action forward – decision after decision after decision. You don't have the luxury of sitting back and getting additional information. The additional information comes from YOU!

Researchers at Harvard have determined that enforcing a time limit on a creative effort can produce faster creative thinking...with one caveat: the team has to be focused on a mission.[35]

---

[35] Amabile, T., Hadley, C. N., & Kramer, S. J. (2002, August 1). Creativity Under the Gun. Retrieved February 8, 2016, from https://hbr.org/2002/08/creativity-under-the-gun/ar/1.

Think of the Apollo 13 ground crew when they had to figure out how to remove the carbon dioxide onboard with extremely limited materials on a badly damaged spacecraft – and then get that spacecraft home! Or the more recent trend of "puzzle rooms" that have grown in popularity in Japan and the U.S. Small groups get locked in a room with puzzles that they have to solve in order to get out of the room. They all have to work on the mission together to escape, and they have to do it in under an hour. Time boxing sets the boundaries needed to move things forward.

It's important not to confuse "time boxing" with "time pressure." Time pressure is that relentless clock at work that is forcing you to complete things by a certain time. "I need that budget by tomorrow." "You'd better get this deployed by Friday or you're fired." "Our customers need this yesterday!"

Time boxing, on the other hand, is the process of:

- Identifying a creative challenge clearly and concisely

- Providing a physical space where people can be devoted only to that task

- Giving a hard and fast time limit

- Trusting the decision or solution that emerges

When All Else Fails, Stand Up

Have you ever noticed that the typical meeting, brainstorming session or problem solving workshop begins with everyone *sitting*? Why IS that?

Well, we aren't really sure. But think about it: where do you do your best thinking? Is it sitting in an uncomfortable chair staring blankly into a computer screen or at a blank piece of paper? Our guess is NO. You, like many others, probably get your "aha" moments when showering, driving in your car, exercising, walking, cooking, etc.

A recent study at Washington University in St. Louis analyzed the group performance of 214 undergraduate students. As part of the study, they divided the students into groups of 3-5 (giving them 54 groups to study). Then they asked each group to complete a creativity task. Half of the groups were directed to a conference room in which there were a table and chairs. The other half had only the table, which forced the team to remain standing. They found that the teams that were standing were not only creative, they were more collaborative![36]

Even just walking can make a difference. People like Jack Dorsey of Twitter, Steve Jobs of Apple, and Mark Zuckerberg of Facebook swear by the "walking meeting." Researchers at Stanford University found that people were more creative after spending time walking. This makes some sense. Think about what has to happen in the brain when you're walking. Various different subsystems need to engage – systems that are related to breathing, balance, and pacing. Some researchers suspect that by distracting those parts of the brain, you allow creative thought to come through.[37] Sound familiar?

[36] Knight, A. P., Baer, M. (2014, November 1). Get Up, Stand Up: The Effects of a Non-Sedentary Workspace on Information Elaboration and Group Performance. Social Psychological and Personality Science, 5(8), 910-917. Retrieved February 8, 2016.

[37] Oppezzo, M., Schwartz, D. L. (2014). Give Your Ideas Some Legs: The Positive Effect of Walking on Creative Thinking. Journal of Experimental Psychology, 40(4), 1142-1152.

Does this mean you should have all of your meetings walking or standing? Probably not. But you might want to try changing things up a bit. For example, consider the following:

- Try a new space for your meetings – in a coffee shop, in a hallway, or in the kitchen

- Hand out white board pens as people walk into a conference room and force them all to stand

- Take a walk around your office or outside while you talk

- Better yet – go gather in the Innovation Room that's discussed in the next subsection!

Innovation Room

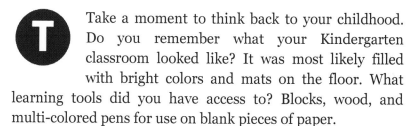 Take a moment to think back to your childhood. Do you remember what your Kindergarten classroom looked like? It was most likely filled with bright colors and mats on the floor. What learning tools did you have access to? Blocks, wood, and multi-colored pens for use on blank pieces of paper.

Now think of your average conference room – what's in there? A table. Chairs. Maybe some inspirational quotes on the walls, if you're lucky. And what tools do you have? Pens. A notebook of lined paper. A laptop and projector...

Guess which one is better for creativity?

Yes, **_we all need to return to our Kindergartner roots_**.

The Innovation Room is space in your offices that you set aside with the sole purpose of inspiring creative thought, supporting brainstorming sessions, stimulating intelligent conversation, and stirring up the hum-drum atmosphere that can pervade workspaces.

If you don't have one, we recommend that you create one as soon as possible.

You should look to your teams to be part of the creation of this environment (and remember to keep the "yes, and..." approach while doing so). Think of what you want this room to be. Ask the following questions:

- Do you envision easy teaming and collaboration?

- Do you want access to multi-media and digital support?

- Do you want to encourage play? Is it meditative? Both?

You and your teams have a fantastic opportunity to develop a space for all employees to break out of the mundane. It can even change during the day – starting out as one space before work, converting to another space during business hours, and becoming a completely new space at the end of the day. Think of the possibilities!

The following design aspects are ideas for customizing your Innovation Room to get you started. Consider:

- *Lighting:* Warm or cool, bright or dim, or any of the above based on timed settings, your room's lighting source(s) will be a huge factor in determining the feel of the area.

- *Texture/Fabrics/Tactile nature:* Strong lines, metal, plastic, or wood? Soft curves with fabric, pillows, floor seating? Walls that are sound-proofed with spongy memory foam? Why not?

- **Colors:** You want to replicate the ocean? How about the mountains? Space? Your choice.

- **Furniture:** From pillows to chairs to overstuffed couches, the possibilities are endless. Red mats for naptime? Treadmills or bouncy balls? A pool table? Pinball machine?

- **Temperature:** Creating a room that is automated to accommodate changes in temperature can be tricky, but having a space that is uncomfortable and takes you out of your "element" can be counter-productive to the room's intent.

- **View:** Windows or none? Some spaces won't be able to offer a view, and that's ok. Deciding whether it is an important component of your design is something you need to do early on. It's also important to keep in mind that you may not want staff peeking in on folks in the room, so think about privacy shades or etched glass to support those inside.

- **Location:** Keep in mind that the location of this space is very important. If your staff can't easily access it, or it will be disruptive to a typically quiet work area, you might want to rethink it.

- **Games:** There are a truckload of inspiring games out there for this room to house. Silly Putty, Jenga, Legos, Mancala, etc. Invest in them.

- **Music/Sound:** Do you want speakers so that your staff can have a dance party? Or a bunch of Beats headphones so they can escape into their own world and jam? New age music? Nature sounds? Rock or alternative at lunch?

- *Food/Beverages:* Nourishing the body is as important as nourishing the mind. Protein bars, nuts, fruit, juices, teas, coffees. Providing quality treats in this space is a good idea. Think of time lost in offices when staff leave to go to their local coffee shop. We aren't saying you need to chain their ankles to their desks here, just remember that if you build it, they will come.

- *Reading materials:* Set aside some space to stack books and magazines you want your staff to have access to while in the Innovation Room. If you are a biomedical engineering firm, it doesn't have to be all medical device mags. The point is to inspire your teams when they are in this room. They probably already know about what's in *Biomedical Engineering Today*. What they need is the book or magazine that's offering ideas about how to think, strategize, create, or become agile and lean. Like, say, *THIS* book!

Of course, these are all just ideas – some will work for your company, and some won't. Don't get tricked into thinking you need a massive budget to get it going. Just like the Implement stage in the 4i Methodology, you just need to start with *something.* Start small, and grow it when you can.

However, make the Innovation Room a priority for your teams. Giving them a space where they can go to be creative can make a huge difference. We promise.

Final Thoughts

Nothing is stronger than habit.

– Ovid

So, what comes next? How do you take this information and begin building your own culture of innovation within your company? We're certain that you won't be surprised by the answer: it depends.

We mentioned in the Introduction that **innovation takes time**. Everyone has to learn, understand and play from the same rulebook before you'll truly see any major change. This is not a "read a book and everything will be fine" approach. You have to practice.

There are many things that can influence your ability to create a culture of innovation – things like: your organizational design, where you and your company are on the innovation continuum, and how much improvisational collaboration is already occurring.

That said, our recommendation is that **you shouldn't go this alone**. What we've found works best is to:

- Get **everyone** trained in the Brain Disruption® process

- Do the train-the-trainer approach and designate in-office trainers who become certified to teach the Brain Disruption 4i Methodology to moderate brainstorming sessions and manage on-going training for new employees

- Perform quarterly "tune-ups" for your trainers so that they can stay up-to-date with new methods and practices

- Perform a culture analysis and find out where your gaps are in your various teams

Most importantly, *just get started.*

The Brain Disruption approach *democratizes innovation.* Anyone and everyone can do it. Everyone has great ideas. That next big breakthrough is just around the corner, as long as you change HOW you innovate – from your brain, to your team, your corporate culture, to your methodology.

With everyone following the same rules, there's no telling *WHAT* radical innovation you'll come up with next.

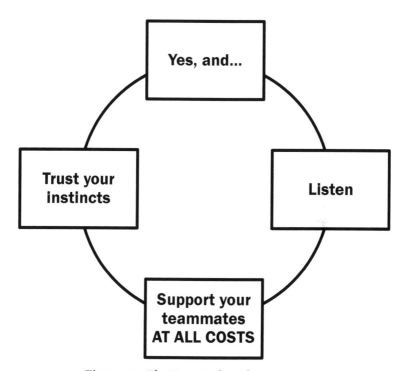

Figure 33: The Four Rules of Improv

Appendix

One Month Brain Disruption Training

You'll be surprised to see your ability to come up with new ideas increases dramatically if you commit 5-10 minutes a day for the next thirty days and perform the following exercises. As we've outlined throughout this book, ***practicing is key*** to changing neural pathways and significantly altering conditioned brain patterns.

The training consists of several different exercises, all of which are described in detail later in this Appendix. They are:

- Alternate Uses Test (AUT)
- Similar Uses Test (SUT)
- Remote Associates Test (RAT)
- Incomplete Figure Test (IFT)
- Riddles

For the best results, use the table below as the schedule for the next four weeks. Where appropriate, chart your results from day to day.

	Mon	Tues	Wed	Thurs	Fri
Week 1	AUT	SUT	RAT	IFT	RIDDLE
Week 2	RAT	RIDDLE	SUT	AUT	IFT
Week 3	SUT	IFT	AUT	RIDDLE	RAT
Week 4	IFT	AUT	RIDDLE	RAT	SUT

Figure 34: Brain Disruption Training Schedule

Exercise 1: Alternate Uses Test (AUT)

Time: approximately 4 minutes

Steps: This exercise is similar to the exercise we performed at the beginning of this book. Take an everyday object and think of as many different uses for it other than the use of intended design. Example objects could include: business card, stapler, picture frame, scissors, or a computer keyboard.

Here's the first one to get you started (see Figure 35). Over the next two minutes think of as many different ways that you can use a **coffee cup** as possible. Go.

Different Ways to Use a Coffee Cup	
1)	11)
2)	12)
3)	13)
4)	14)
5)	15)
6)	16)
7)	17)
8)	18)
9)	19)
10)	20)

Figure 35: Different Ways to Use a Coffee Cup

Debrief: You will find that some days have far better results than others. Rate yourself, and list why you think you performed the way you did. See if you can identify patterns for both good days and bad days. Things to consider include:

- What was your frame of mind when you started?
- Were you hungry or well fed?
- Was there bad traffic?
- Was there noise distracting you?

Exercise 2: Similar Uses Test (SUT)

**Time:** Approximately 4 minutes

**Steps:** This exercise is similar to the AUT in that you're going to use an everyday object from around your office. Pick an object, say a file cabinet. Next, define what the object does, its function. "A file cabinet is designed to hold paper." Now take two minutes and list as many different objects that are designed to do the same thing. You might come up with: briefcase, photocopier, wrapping for a ream of paper, FedEx box, envelope, Iron Mountain storage.

Note: like the AUT, don't be limited be the size or shape of the object, be creative as to how you define the function of the object. If you picked staple remover, you could define the object as "to remove staples," or as "to pinch at another object to remove something." Which function do you think will get you more creative results?

Take two minutes and use "bookshelf" as your object.

Similar Uses for a Bookshelf	
1)	11)
2)	12)
3)	13)
4)	14)
5)	15)
6)	16)
7)	17)
8)	18)
9)	19)
10)	20)

Figure 36: Similar Uses for a Bookshelf

Debrief: As with the AUT, you will find that some days have far better results than others. Rate yourself, and list why you think you performed the way you did. See if you can identify patterns for both good days and bad days. Things to consider include:

- What was your frame of mind when you started?
- Were you hungry or well fed?
- Was there bad traffic?
- Was there noise distracting you?

Exercise 3: Remote Associates Test (RAT)

Time: approximately 8 minutes

Steps: The Remote Associates Test (RAT) was developed by Sarnoff Mednick in the 1960s as a test used to measure creative thinking. The RAT asks you to come up with the word that links a selection of other words. For example, what connects the following words: Paint / Doll / Cat? The answer: house (house paint, dollhouse, cathouse).

Giving yourself 8 minutes, look at the table below and find the associations – the common word that binds them together. (Answers are at the end of the Appendix)

Items	_Answer_
1) Square / Cardboard / Open	
2) Broken / Clear / Eye	
3) Coin / Quick / Spoon	
4) Time / Hair / Stretch	
5) Land / Hand / House	
6) Hungry / Order / Belt	
7) Way / Ground / Weather	
8) Sore / Shoulder / Sweat	

Figure 37: Remote Associates Test (RAT)

Exercise 4: Incomplete Figure Test

Time: approximately 4 minutes

Steps: This exercise is pure creativity and "out-of-the-box" thinking. One of the most iconic elements of the Torrance Test for Creative Thought (TTCT) is the Incomplete Figure test, a drawing challenge.

1)   Give yourself five minutes to see what you can turn them in to. Uncommon subject matter, implied stories, humor, and original perspective all earn high marks.

2)   See examples below for your first two challenges. Go here to find other incomplete figures or have someone create a few for you, like your child or co-worker. (We used to play a game with our kids as they were growing up that is exactly like this – we called it the "doodle game" – one person would create a fairly simple doodle and the other person had to make something out of it. As they got older, we applied some rules to it to stretch ourselves such as NO FACES...)

3)   Now, giving yourself 5 minutes, look at the figure and open your mind to the possibilities of what it could be. Turn the page around. Envision it as filled in, or a small part of something much bigger.

Note: Many of our clients struggle with this exercise as it's been awhile since they did some serious doodling. Maybe take the first minute to allow for many ideas instead of settling on the first instinct. You may find yourself eventually going back to that idea as the final decision, and that's totally fine. It's just a good idea to not lock yourself in too early. Think of the possibilities!

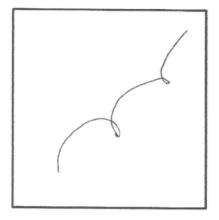

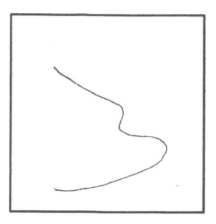

Figure 38: Incomplete Figure Test

See the last page for an example.

Exercise 5:Riddles

Time: approximately 5 minutes

Steps: You may remember reading Tolkien novels or playing around with riddles when you were younger. Here's one that we remember from "*The Hobbit.*"

A box without hinges, key or lid,

Yet golden treasure inside is hid.

Answer: Egg

Now here's one for you. Take up to 10 minutes to answer the following riddle. Remember to allow yourself to stay open minded and avoid locking in or forcing an answer to fit. Of course, if you're able to solve it quickly, that's great! Also, don't beat yourself up if you struggle to identify it right away – the point is to give your brain that much needed daily workout.

- ***Question:*** We hurt without moving. We poison without touching. We bear the truth and the lies. We are not to be judged by our size. What are we? (the answer is on the last few pages of the book)

You can find more riddles at the following websites:

- www.goodriddlesnow.com

- www.riddlers.org
- http://www.buzzle.com/articles/hard-riddles-for-adults.html

Answers

Remote Associates Test (RAT) – Answers

Items	*Answer*
1) Square / Cardboard / Open	Box
2) Broken / Clear / Eye	Glass
3) Coin / Quick / Spoon	Silver
4) Time / Hair / Stretch	Long
5) Land / Hand / House	Farm
6) Hungry / Order / Belt	Money
7) Way / Ground / Weather	Fair
8) Sore / Shoulder / Sweat	Cold

Figure 39: Remote Associates Test (RAT) – Answers

Riddle

Words.

Here's an example of what you might have come up with for the Incomplete Figure Test.

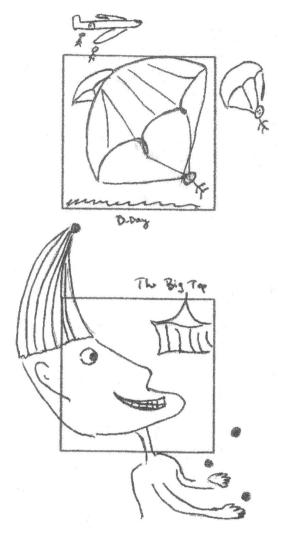

Figure 40: Incomplete Figure Test (example)

ABOUT THE AUTHORS

Bruce and Gail started ExperienceYes in 2013 and have been quickly building their client base in the fields of telecom, education, oil & gas, healthcare, and management consulting. They both still nurture their passion for performing staying busy with local theatre companies, such as The Evergreen Players and the Evergreen Players improv Comedy troupe (EPiC).

They are married, have two teen-aged children, and live in Evergreen, CO. You can find out more about them on their website http://www.ExperienceYes.com or on Facebook at facebook.com/ExperienceYes.

Made in the USA
San Bernardino, CA
19 March 2016